Dedicated to Adele Rice Nudel and
David Nudel, my sister and brother-
in-law; Claire Murphy; Isabel
Flanagan; Elsie Ludlow; Kathleen
Swords Villafaña; and Elizabeth Frank.

Acknowledgments

I would especially like to thank Madeline Ward, Bill Philip, Lloyd McCraney and Ed Myers, who gave me encouragement; my sister, Adele Rice Nudel, author of *For the Woman Over Fifty* (Avon), who gave me love and lifted my spirits when they were down; Elizabeth Frank, who was always there; the worldwide fellowships of Al-Anon, Al-Ateen, and Alcoholics Anonymous, who are always there for anyone who needs them; Dr. Francis Soper and Dr. Ernest Steed, who believed in this book; and Ron Lawson, who helped me keep up my faith.

GETTING THEM SOBER

Volume 1

TOBY RICE DREWS

author of
"Get Rid of Anxiety and Stress"

BRIDGE PUBLISHING, INC.
South Plainfield, N.J. 07080
Publishers of:
LOGOS • HAVEN • OPEN SCROLL

Also by Toby Rice Drews:

Getting Them Sober, Volume Two
Getting Them Sober, Volume One—Action Guide
Get Rid of Anxiety and Stress

GETTING THEM SOBER
Copyright © 1980 by Logos International
All rights reserved
Printed in the United States of America
Library of Congress Catalog Card Number: 80-82751
International Standard Book Number: 0-88270-460-5
Logos International, Plainfield, New Jersey 07060

Foreword

Reading this book helped me understand *why* the wives go back to batterers and *why* they drop the charges after taking out the warrants. But most important, it has helped me to understand so thoroughly that I am able to *use* the ideas and program in this book to reach these family members, to convince them to go into counseling, to convince them to take the next necessary steps that will heal them and their families.

I wholeheartedly recommend this book as reading for professionals who deal with families of alcoholics—*and I recommend it to those families*. This book has the unique ability to relate on *all* levels; family members of any age can read it and follow it. But it is deceptively simple. The theories and solutions are new, complex and effective. *and are from Alanon!* Professionals will welcome it as a workable counseling aid.

I will keep copies of it next to the Bench to give to families in crises. I recommend that other judges do the same for prevention and treatment of this horrible disease called alcoholism. In this way, even if an alcoholic's family does not follow through for counseling, they will get a lot of help, support and suggestions by reading. I believe any family member who reads this book will be positively affected by it and be able, finally, to take *some* steps he or she wasn't able to take before.

I strongly feel this book would be a marvelous discussion/action-based tool to use in counseling centers, in alcoholism treatment facilities and in schools.

It's a gentle book; it totally accepts the family and its rage, guilt and wavering of action; it understands it all and helps family members to finally make moves they couldn't before.

Other books in the field have recommended some of the ideas of this book. But most members of an alcoholic's family have not been able to make the jump to *doing them. What makes this book different?* The author intimately knows what fears an alcoholic's family is living under. She knows the "clubs" the alcoholic uses to make the family seem like "the controllers," the "bad guys," the "ones who never love them enough." She knows the *hidden* fears that keep the wife from acting—see, for example, Chapter 40, "Don't Be Scared That He Will Leave if He Gets Well." The author takes the reader by the hand and gently teaches her how to go past her husband's *alcoholic threats*—past his arrogance, his *crazy-making*—and on to live a peaceful, productive, sane life.

And, in the course of all this, she shows that if the family follows the program involved, it helps the alcoholic to have an 80 percent better chance to get sober and stay sober.

I believe this book is *must* reading for all families of alcoholics—and anyone who cares about helping them.

> The Honorable Robert B. Watts,
> Supreme Bench Judge, Baltimore City
> Executive Board Member, Baltimore
> Area Council on Alcoholism

Author's Foreword

You feel you don't need to read this book because you haven't lived with an alcoholic—or because you no longer live with an alcoholic?

In Alcoholics Anonymous they say that alcoholism is an insidious, baffling and cunning disease. The effects of the disease are even more insidious and devastating to members of the alcoholic's family than they are to the alcoholic. This disease is so powerful that it *creates* terrible personality changes in members of the alcoholic's family. These effects do not just "go away" after the alcoholic is no longer present in the home.

vo!

A person doesn't have to grow up with alcoholism in his family in order to carry the scars of that disease around. If you've lived with alcoholism for any length of time, I believe you have a hidden infection—one that you may believe is gone for good—but is actually ready to act up again in you.

no

the alcoholism

Most women who are, or were, married to alco-

(and alcoholics)

Alcoholism does ~~not~~ *create co-alco-holics. Their illness is their own!*

holics—and are now apart from them through death, divorce or separation—say to themselves, "Well! I'll never go through that again!"

Is that true? Statistics prove otherwise. *If untreated for alcoholism's effects on her* [co-alcoholism], *the wife will often marry an alcoholic again—and not even realize she is doing so, until it's too late.*

What are the effects of her ~~former husband's alcoholism in her life~~ [co-alcoholism]—the effects that set her up to marry yet another alcoholic? They are found in the ["Co"] behavior patterns she learned to practice ~~while married to an alcoholic~~ [in childhood] [due to her personality]—patterns she probably does not even realize she has learned. She will probably repeat these patterns with her new husband.

What are these behavior patterns? If I had to choose one that invariably characterizes this kind of woman—the kind who is drawn to needy men—it would be the neurotic need to prove to him *how good she is for him* and her overlooking whether or not he is truly good for her. ✳

This is a compulsive need on her part—the need to be his counselor, best cook, sexiest partner, anything and everything he wants and needs (she even anticipates his needs) at any time of night or day. She is frantic in her drive to show him she will always be centered around him. She wants him to stay with her.

The friend of a woman with this need may suggest, "Why don't you take your time to be sure he is as good for you as you feel you will be for him?"

✳ Her Addiction is an obsessive "need to be needed". She is a dependent PEOPLE addict.

Mentally dismissing this advice, the woman may respond, "But you don't know how sensitive he is. He is truly extraordinary and we are very close. He even trusts me with his deepest thoughts."

Sensing her counselee's anxiety, the friend will probably point out, "Sometimes I think you question your ability to develop a lasting relationship with a man who is kind to you, a man who gives of himself—and I don't want to see you make the same mistake twice."

Again, the advice goes unheeded, and almost unheard, until it comes crashing back into the woman's thoughts—months or years later.

Does this make you wince? Are you dating a needy, sensitive man? If you're scared that this road might lead only to hell, you're right. If you think you've plunged so deep that you can't, and don't even want to get out, you're wrong. *You don't have to want to—you just have to want to want to, eventually. You just have to want to wind up so sick and tired of being hurt that you get to the point of wanting a man who is good to you, instead of being in this same predicament ten years later, ten years older.*

But what do you do *today?* Here are some suggestions:

1. Try to remember that there are over 1½ billion men on earth. *He's not your last-chance Charlie.*

2. Loneliness does not have to be devastating. While

you are changing your behavior, you will go through some times alone. Try to put that period of time in its true perspective.

3. Fill up your time with creative and joyful people and events, instead of soap-opera fantasies. Investigate and uncover your talents and interests and expand your horizons.

4. A few weeks or months of not having such intensity in a relationship will be very good for you. Each time you learn to act as if you are valuable, not desperate, you make it easier the next time. *And that's the way you must learn to act, to get a man who will value you.*

5. Again, maintain a realistic perspective on life. It's not as difficult, nor as exciting, as you sometimes *feel*. Take it slow and easy.

Contents

Introduction

Alcoholism isn't just drinking.

It's a *family* disease. It causes the wife and kids to become as addicted to the alcoholic as the alcoholic is to the booze.

While the alcoholic lies passed out, anesthetized, his family goes through the years of his drinking— stark, raving sober. Their world is like no sane family's world. They believe lies, expect miracles, have him locked up, bail him out, wish he were dead, and pray that he gets home safely.

Sobriety, too, is a family affair.

Yes, it's true that he has to want to get sober before he will ever get sober.* But there's a lot the family can do to help promote the best atmosphere to enable the alcoholic to *want* sobriety.

Following the suggestions in this book won't guarantee sobriety for the alcoholic—*but if the wife of the alcoholic changes her behavior, as outlined in this book, the alcoholic has an 80 percent better chance to get sober than before.*

Where does that statistic come from? This book

This is an aspect of co-alcoholic "denial" within the counseling field or counselors are frequently co-alcoholics.

called "Counseling the Co-Alcoholic"

Al-anon green-
work!

* *This fosters the notion that the families job is to help the alcoholic rather than heal their own addiction. This may be a good idea at the beginning of counseling but must soon change if the family is to heal. See*

xv

incorporates the best of all known therapies for the family of the alcoholic—therapies that have been tried and tested all over the world with over one million family members. These principles work. *(This speaking of Alanon)*

This book will show you how to handle hundreds *not* of situations that come up in a relationship with an *therapy* alcoholic—situations that have always "thrown" you. And it will show you how to handle such circumstances in ways that eliminate your guilt, and yet take into account your very normal feelings of rage.

It will teach you how to cope, not just for a moment, but over a sustained period of time, and how to clear your head and begin to make rational decisions again. It won't tell you, perhaps like a well-meaning friend might do, to "throw the bum out." Only *you* know what you can live with and what you can't. On the other hand, I know you don't need any more outsiders telling you to "stop attacking that poor guy" and to "get yourself together."

You need support. You need information about what alcoholism is, and what it is doing and will do to your whole family.

This book gives direct advice about what you can do in specific situations, step-by-step directions on how to accomplish your goals and the results you can expect when you begin to make these changes.

Your reading can open the way to a new beginning for you. The changes suggested here are difficult, yet simple. No one can do them all—overnight. You can keep a record of your progress. Learn to write down your feelings, your reactions, to be able to see them from a distance. Above all, be gentle with yourself. See every change you make in your behavior—even if it only lasts five minutes—as a building block.

After making the changes outlined in this book, you will find yourself living a sane and serene life *whether your alcoholic is still drinking or not.* This is a promise.

NOTE: This book is written for men and women. We have not used both masculine and feminine pronouns throughout the book, however, because this would be impractical and distracting. If you are a husband of a woman alcoholic, please substitute "he" for "she" and vice versa, because the principles of this book pertain to individuals involved with alcoholism, regardless of their gender.

1

No More Taking the Blame for His Drinking!

You cannot cause anyone to drink.
You cannot control anyone's drinking.
You cannot cure anyone's drinking.

You probably feel guilty or resentful so much of the time that it's a long time since you did not experience these feelings. These emotions are very normal for a person in your circumstances.

When the alcoholic acts rotten, you feel like a resentful saint. For example, sometimes out of the blue, when things are going well, you seem to say something that "triggers" the alcoholic to blow up and get a drink. Or you overreact all the time to everything he says or does because you've got so many pent-up feelings of frustration. When this happens, the alcoholic reaches for the bottle or goes slamming out the door to the bar.

"It's all your fault!" he accuses. You've heard it so often, and more than likely you believe it by now

The alcoholic needs you to keep believing this so he can dump the responsibility for his drinking on you.

Are you responsible for the drinking?

Look at it in this light: Can you make a tubercular patient cough? Can you make him stop coughing? Tuberculosis is a disease. Alcoholism is a disease. *You* cannot cause, control or cure a disease. You cannot make your alcoholic drink; neither can you make him stop. *He* bends his elbow; he makes the choice. Always remember this.

What can you do when he accuses you—or when his family accuses you—of causing him to drink? When you feel capable of speaking calmly, say this (only once—they'll really hear you that way): "I am not responsible for anyone's drinking. If he chooses to drink, that's his business."

Then, simply be quiet. Leave the room if you have to in order to avoid an argument. You don't ever have to discuss it again. They'll get the idea.

What will this accomplish? Once you really start to believe you are not responsible for his behavior, you will no longer be able to be emotionally blackmailed. You'll stop feeling guilty and you'll stop thinking you need to be punished for making your alcoholic drink. And probably for the first time in his life, the alcoholic will feel that someone is saying, "I love you enough to let you grow up and be responsible for your own life."

God, give me the courage to cope with the situation that threatens to rob my peace of mind.

2

Be Gentle With Yourself

Give yourself credit for small successes.
You are not a failure as a wife when you are angry.
Living with an alcoholic is too much for most people.

It's hard to do anything right during a crisis. And crises happen very regularly in an alcoholic's home. When things are going well for a few hours, or a day or so (if you're lucky), your alcoholic will pull another "zinger" and it's like you had forgotten how terrible things could be. Once again you had settled into believing he might really get well *this time*. Whammo, it happens all over again. Then he even denies his drinking problem, and you get furious, depressed and begin to believe *you're* the crazy one.

This is the time to stop, and think. You must learn to say to yourself, "This is a crisis. I am not crazy. It *is* happening. There is a way out of the trap. Maybe it is not the whole answer, right now. But I am going to do one small thing that can calm *me* down, at least for half an hour or so during all this mess."

Don't get the idea I'm telling you to calm down for him. Neither am I saying you should learn how to put up with his "stuff," and even be calm about it! Instead, I am saying that when an alcoholic's wife screams at her husband or hits him, she generally experiences guilt, even if it is unconscious. This causes her to feel *she's* the persecutor of this "poor guy." He likes her to feel guilty about getting angry, because it keeps her in the same old predictable rut—screaming, yelling, throwing, crying, *but not changing anything, really.*

This is a typical pattern: You become infuriated by what he does, and then you punish him by becoming enraged or not speaking. He proceeds to give his hangdog look, and maybe cries some tears of remorse, begs for forgiveness, etc., *ad nauseum.* His performance makes you feel like you've beaten a baby. How can you possibly keep your promise to yourself, then, of "not taking this any more"? You're guilt-ridden enough, from "punishing" him. So how do you get out of the rut?

You must learn a new behavior. When he does "his thing"—try not to retaliate. Leave the room, meditate, breathe a prayer, tune him out, whatever. You need to maintain a safe distance, almost a detachment, from him. The next step is to *think calmly about what a rational person would do.* Don't yell and thereby set yourself up for a guilt trip which will prevent you from leaving or doing whatever it takes to keep from being manipulated by his nonsense.

This is no time to make a pronouncement. When you are really calm, later, and have thought out your plan of action, simply proceed to do it. This requires no discussion; you do not need to explain to your alcoholic or ask his permission or get his approval for your refusing to accept his unacceptable behavior any more.

Once you succeed in not overreacting, your unconscious mind will be free of guilt—and at this point you will be *free* to be truly rational and make logical decisions about what you're going to do.

Most counselors get very frustrated by the battered wife (most wives of alcoholics are battered) who continually goes back to her husband. It's a baffling situation. The counselor may wonder, "How can she forget reality so quickly?" The answer is that the wife is used to years of two self-punishments: her own denial that typically takes this form, "It will be better next time, truly it will." Or this: "I'm so mean; I've punished him by my words and yelling. Maybe if I go back and *I* change—maybe if *I* learn not to yell—" Frequently, an alcoholic's wife believes she is the cause of his behavior. Of course she should learn how not to get upset—*but it is for her sake, not for his. It will help her lessen her guilt so she will be able to decide sanely whether to leave or stay.*

Get away from feeling responsible for him. *He loves that.* If you stay in that trap, you'll stay angry and baffled and depressed. *You've got to change your behavior for your sanity—to keep out of doctors' offices or hospitals. To keep yourself free from stomach, back, headache, and gynecological problems that happen as a result of living with insanity.*

If, in the process of your getting calm enough to make rational decisions about how to best live so that you can get some peace in your life, your alcoholic decides to get sober too, fine. If not, you've lost nothing by finding peace for yourself! There is no use in both of you going down the tubes. Save yourself. Be gentle on you. You've been through a lot. You need nurturing and pampering. Give it to yourself.

Above all, remember you must learn to protect yourself emotionally and learn it is your right not to place your psyche in the hands of an insane person. He is sick, but you're not here on earth to be battered by a sick man. *It doesn't help him to be able to hurt you. In fact, it makes him sicker.* If you will learn to take care and be gentle with yourself, you will be helping him, in the highest sense of help.

Keeping all this in mind, I know you will be better able to be gentle with yourself. Trying to get sane, in the middle of living with craziness, is as hard as getting sober in a bar. Your setbacks do not make you a failure; they can motivate you on to success

Just remember to take care of yourself.

Help me, Lord, to see myself in the light of your unconditional love.

3

Don't Worry About Whether He's Really an Alcoholic

If it's that much of a problem, he probably is.
If he's drinking that much now, he's probably in the early stages of alcoholism.
Social drinkers don't usually upset their families with their drinking.

Many wives of alcoholics ask me if their husbands are really alcoholics. This usually happens during the initial counseling session.

Here is one such interview: "But—suppose he's not really an alcoholic? *Then* what do I do?"

"Just the same as you would if he were. But—let's back up. What makes you think he might not be an alcoholic?"

"Well, he's kept his job for almost twenty years. His friends certainly get drunk more often than him. He goes for days without drinking. One time, he even stopped for four months." She counted them off on her fingers. "Isn't that a long time for an alcoholic to be without a drink?"

"Annie," I told her, "take a look at these twenty questions to see if you think he's really an alcoholic." (The list is at the back of this book.) "Can you truthfully say that three of them are true of your husband? Yes? Then he *is* an alcoholic. Every known authority in the field of alcoholism agrees that three yeses to these questions means the individual definitely *is* an alcoholic."

Annie didn't want to hear me. After a long, thoughtful pause, she exclaimed, *"But*—I just can't think of him as an alcoholic! It seems too horrible!"

"Look, Annie, this is a crucial point in counseling. You can continue denying and walk out of here right now. But, if you do, the disease will continue; it will get worse and your husband will either die or go crazy. Or you can stay and do things that are hard to do in order to learn how to create the best conditions under which your husband has an optimal chance to get well and stay alive."

Annie was scared, but she stayed to listen.

I went on, "A lot of people don't want to hear the diagnosis when their parent gets cancer. They scream at the doctor. They refuse to face it and consequently they don't do anything about their loved one's condition. The patient doesn't get treatment until much later, when it's all too obvious it's beyond help.

"Fortunately, alcoholism is an arrestable disease— it's not like cancer. That means if your husband stops drinking, the damage to his liver can be arrested; your marriage can be wonderful again. He can live long and have a productive life. See, Annie? Saying he has alcoholism *isn't* like pronouncing his death sentence. Putting your head in the sand by believing, in effect, "If I say it's not there, it'll go away" is what children do when they're scared. But *you* can handle this. You're an adult."

"But if he loved me, wouldn't he stop?"

"Let's get back to the disease concept of alcoholism. If a diabetic loved you, would that mean he stopped being allergic to sugar? You see, your husband is a drug addict. He's allergic to, and addicted to, a drug: alcohol. He can't stop right now. He's too scared to stop. But it you follow the basic directions of this book, you'll find he has a good chance to choose—to want—sobriety!

"Annie, alcoholism is a family disease. *You can see what it's doing to him—but can you see what it's doing to you?*"

Annie then began to open up. She poured out all the things he'd been doing to her, to the kids, and to himself. Her appearance was as ravaged as any alcoholic who just walked into a treatment center. She was shaking, drawn-looking, exhausted; she had been in a three-year-long depression.

She wanted to believe he could learn to *control* his drinking, and she figured he'd have a chance to 'make it' if someone could show him how to control it.

11

"Annie, there's a lot of hope here too. There are over one and a half million people, now sober, in Alcoholics Anonymous. They don't drink—at all. They know they *can't* drink, ever. And they do it, one day at a time. The point is that their wives, their spouses, too, thought they would never be able to do that. *But they are successful!* If you do what *you're* supposed to do, to help *yourself*—that *will* be helping him too. This gives him an 80 percent better chance to choose sobriety than if you don't do these things. He has an 80 percent better chance to choose to go to A.A. and stay alive if you *really* help, the right way. And the 'right way' means doing all the things that will help you to feel good about yourself—just the opposite of all the self-sacrificing things you've been doing!" I laughed, "Annie, your 'prescription' is to make yourself happy! And that's the best thing you can do for your husband! Now that's not a rotten thing for a counselor to advise, is it?"

She laughed, but went on to tell me, "He's never going to admit to being an alcoholic."

"He doesn't have to—to you or me. When he's hurting bad enough—and when it's the right time— he'll get help. And he might not even say he's an alcoholic for a long time, even after he's on treatment! He might just tell the guys in A.A., or the doctor, or whomever, that he has a little problem with his drinking. Who he admits it to is not important, right away. What's important is that he'll get treatment. And as they say, 'A.A. spoils their drinking!' "

"What do you mean?"

"Right now he probably thinks he's having fun. Believe me, Annie, after he attends one or two A.A. meetings and hears those talks about what drinking leads to, he will get so scared of his disease that it will totally spoil his illusion that alcohol is fun.

"And most important: Is his drinking upsetting you? If it is, it really doesn't matter if we call it alcoholism. Begin to do the things we are talking about here whether or not you think he's an alcoholic, got a drinking problem, or whatever. I believe anyone working in the field of alcoholism would take one look at you, hear about his drinking, and call his condition 'alcoholism.' Annie, you're not crazy—you just live with alcoholism. That's why you feel crazy. Do the things we talked about and you'll stop *feeling* crazy; you'll start to feel good and peaceful and calm—very, very soon."

God I thank you for allowing me to see that alcoholism is a disease for which there is hope.

4

Don't Pour Out the Booze

He'll get more—doesn't he always?
It costs too much to replace it.
(It's your budget too.)

Mae was a tall, energetic woman who, even after twenty-five years of marriage to Phil, her alcoholic husband, had a great deal of enthusiasm for life. But she was beginning to look harried, drawn. For the past five years, she had managed to do quite well, keeping an emotional distance from her husband. He was drinking in bars most of the time. Then Phil's condition changed, physically. His illness progressed and he couldn't get outside like he used to. He was too weakened, too tired. Besides, he had temporarily lost his driver's license after his third encounter with the police, "driving while drinking." And his favorite bars were too far away to walk to.

Years ago Mae had gone through her period of jealousy and feelings of deprivation and loneliness when her husband drank at the bars every night. But she adjusted, because she wanted to stay with him for various reasons at that time. So not to go crazy, she blocked out a life of her own and built a "bubble" around herself, emotionally, causing her feelings of anxiety and rage to be submerged. She channeled her energies into her kids, her job, her aging mother, her church work. They lived a life of *détente*, a somewhat peaceful coexistence, accepting the fact that that if she wanted him there—and she did—then it had to be on *his* terms.

Mae really did believe things would go on like this, *forever*. She always thought he would keep his job, drink, come home, pass out, and, if she stayed out of his way, there'd be some kind of animal comfort in knowing he'd be home at night, eventually.

She even stopped feeling jealous when she read about alcoholism and how most men, after drinking as long as her husband had, were much more interested in the bottle than a woman—even when they acted like that wasn't so. And even if he did become interested in the female on the next bar stool, he probably couldn't stay conscious long enough to have a sexual encounter—or even be potent enough to start one. Besides, he was really too afraid to even try, thinking he'd probably fail. That part of his life—and his pathetic attempts to still try to occasionally scare Mae about the "other women"—had long lost their effect on her.

But Mae forgot about the fact that the disease of alcoholism is a progressive one. She often thought about it being fatal, and she vacillated between sometimes wishing he would just die, so it'd be over with and she'd have some peace—and feeling scared and sorry for him, that he would die if he didn't stop. She was frightened for herself at being left entirely alone, and experienced nagging guilt over her thoughts and feelings.

She knew alcoholism is progressive, but she didn't think it would happen so soon. You see, one of the illusions Mae swallowed when her husband acted like he was so powerful for so many years had the effect of making Mae believe her husband was as invincible to this disease's progression as he said he was. Oh, he often claimed that if he didn't stop, it would "get him too." But he *really* didn't believe that, way down deep, most of the time. He was scared and he kept trying to convince himself—and act like—*he had forever*.

As the sign says in some alcoholism detoxification units,

WE DON'T HAVE TIME TO TAKE OUR TIME.

An alcoholic often believes he truly has all the time in the world to finally make that decision to surrender his sickness, to give it up. He often, when still committed to it, believes he can somehow finally outwit that very cunning, baffling and powerful alcoholism.

And wives often despair because they have also

believed this illusion. "God protects drunks and fools," so goes the old myth—the myth that perpetuates the idea that the alcoholic can slide by, can stay at one stage of the disease and just hide there, just hang in there without going further, without *truly* getting well.

That's the illusion Mae and Phil were living under.

She even hoped, much of the time, that things would stay the same, not change, not get worse. She did not realize it would be good for him to "get worse," then, hopefully, he might hurt enough to decide to get well. Both of their hopes in this area were understandable: He was too scared to give it up— yet. She didn't want the boat rocked—it had taken too many years to get this much peace in their home.

But now Phil was home a lot. Drinking at home— at night and on weekends.

Somehow, it had been easier on Mae when she didn't have to see it.

So it started driving her crazy, all over again.

She started to mark the bottles, pour them out, empty half of their contents, hide them, find them and scream and cry and beg him to stop. She stopped spending time with her women friends because she was too busy, always looking for bottles to throw out or pour out.

That's when Mae showed up at the therapy group.

"I thought I had this thing licked. I was coping with it. Our house was calmer. Why did he have to go and get arrested for drunk driving? Why does he have to get physically sicker? And now I have that extra worry about his health, about his ability to keep any job. I can't stand it any more."

I made some suggestions to Mae:

1. Accept that this is a hard time for you. Be very gentle with yourself right now. Treat yourself very lovingly, nurture yourself. Give yourself little splurges—and big ones—when you can afford them. But, certainly, at least, little ones.

2. Try to remember it's really good that he's getting sicker, because it won't drag out forever. When alcoholics start getting sicker, they often start getting better. At least, when he's hurting so bad he just may decide he can't stand it any longer—and decide to get help.

3. Group support is very important for you. You need regular reassurance that it's necessary for you to become detached from his problem. Let him hurt, *do not rescue him*. Let the crises happen—health, jobs, everything. You will need support to prevent you from experiencing guilt and pity for him. Keep your compassion at a distance.

"Remember, you can't save him, even if you want to," I had to tell Mae over and over.

Temporarily "saving" him was only postponing his final surrender to true recovery anyway. So it wasn't really helping.

4. Finally, we gently, but firmly, told Mae: "Don't pour out the booze." I pleaded, "The next bottle you

throw out might be just the one that gets him so sick that he will wind up in a hospital! God forbid that you should prevent that from happening!"

Mae took a vacation at her sister's home, came back refreshed, and was able to leave his bottles to him.

She gave up his problem and she kept her peace of mind.

Her husband? He got so scared by her lack of worry that he signed himself into a hospital!

He's been sober a month now.

Cause me to realize thy loving kindness in the morning, for in thee do I trust.

5

Learn To Relax

Panic is distressing, but not dangerous.
Don't be afraid of being afraid.

If you turned to this page because you are anxious, let me reassure you that you are not alone. Many people experience a great deal of panic when they make major role shifts in their lives—*especially* when they begin to be good to themselves after a lifetime of feeling miserable.

Sara, a bouncy former patient of mine, used to come to her therapy sessions with lists of questions she had written down during the week. All the mental and physical changes she had been experiencing (and they were positive changes!) not only puzzled her, but terrified her. Oh, she looked "all together," but inside, Sara was a nervous wreck. "I'm *doing* everything you say. And I feel worse! I get these 'anxiety attacks' just when everything's going well. I know you said the good feelings will catch up with me later, after I get used to doing good things for myself, but what do I do *now?*! Actually, it's not just when things go well. I get anxious when things are terrible—and then when they begin to go well, I wait for the axe to fall. And I never think it'll just happen in one area of my life. If I get a cold, I think it's the flu, then I imagine dying of complications from pneumonia. I think my husband will lose his job, my boy will drop out of school, and on and on and on. I get so sick of it all. And I can't stop. Then, because I'm nervous, I fall or turn my ankle a little bit and I think I've broken it. I worry about it. I elevate my leg. It starts to get pins and needles in it. Then I think I've got gangrene. No kidding. Or I eat too much because I'm depressed and I get a stomachache. Then, I get nauseous (probably from guilt) and I think the food's been out too long from the refrigerator. I get totally panicked and think I'm going to die and I can't breathe enough air. It's like I'm dying."

Sara's not unusual. She's not crazy either. She's just got a garden-variety neurosis called anxiety. It takes many forms: in some people it manifests itself in headaches, nausea, vomiting, and tingling fingers. Others get diarrhea, or constipation; still others hyperventilate (breathe too rapidly when anxious, causing the anxiety to escalate even further). The symptoms go on and on. Perhaps you've been to the doctor about them—*most wives of alcoholics develop some physical symptoms of stress from living with an alcoholic.* They range from migraine headaches to gynecological problems that won't clear up,

21

to constant fatigue, backache and hypochondria. Living with an alcoholic *is* too much for most people.

What do you do in this situation? First, you must make a decision to put yourself first for a change. And by that, I mean you must place priority on your mental, spiritual, and physical health. For these symptoms are not "silly." You must not ignore them. Constant stomach distress can be a real problem; it could lead to an ulcer, colitis or constant pain.

Even if you are willing to put up with the stress, it will get worse. Constant stress, and its physical side-kicks, have caused many a person to wind up in the hospital for exploratory stomach surgery, only to discover "it's nothing." The doctor just tells you to relax, or to leave the situation that's causing it. Easy to say; hard to do.

Whether you decide to stay or leave, you must learn to *relax*. This means you must give your churning, pained, acid-filled stomach a rest from it all. It means you need to learn how to give your body a chance, every day, to learn how to live pain-free. *It means you may prolong your life another fifteen years*.

A few additional life-saving facts: Relaxation methods save lives of cardiac patients; those who practice them religiously often prevent a second heart attack. Relaxation methods often reduce arthritis pain, help people get off tranquilizers, help smokers quit, reduce the pain of chronic physical disorders, and give regular peace-of-mind breaks from the terrible stress of living with an alcoholic

What causes stomach distress? There is a very simple cause: when you're upset or scared, your body produces Adrenalin. This happens to every person and animal. Ever see a frightened rabbit stand still for a time and then run? That's called the "flight-or-fight" syndrome. You are conditioned either to fight or run. If you do neither, and you bottle up your feelings (wives of alcoholics do this a lot of the time), then your Adrenalin has to "go somewhere." This results in problems with your stomach, back, or head. *It* fights *you*. This process can lead to an "anxiety attack." In addition to the Adrenalin causing painful symptoms, *you get scared of the symptoms and think you're dying*. This fear of the symptoms just increases the amount of Adrenalin you produce and the symptoms get worse—and on and on it goes—a vicious cycle.

Relaxation techniques not only help you get rid of the symptoms, but they cause a break time in your fear of the symptoms and therefore help to wind down your anxiety attacks.

Here is a technique you can use, starting right now. This is the best method! Two times a day sit in an easy chair, dim the lights and seclude yourself from physical distractions and noise for fifteen minutes.

While doing this, close your eyes and clear your mind of all thoughts. *Concentrate* on the parts of your body that are being tensed, then relax. If another anxiety-producing thought creeps into your mind, replace it with thoughts of relaxation. Then follow these simple steps:

1. Put your arms out in front of you and hold them there till the count of five, then drop them.

2. Extend your arms again, then make tense fists till the count of five, then drop them and relax.

3. Hold your arms out once again. This time, stretch your fingers wide to the count of five, then relax and lower them.

4. Next, you should tightly wrinkle your forehead to the count of five, followed by relaxation.

5. Pucker your mouth and tense your jaw to the count of five; relax.

6. Tightly arch your neck to the count of five; relax.

7. Touch your chin to your chest to the count of five; relax.

8. Hunch your shoulders, letting your arms stay relaxed, till the count of five; relax.

9. Tightly arch your back, till the count of five; relax.

10. Hold your stomach in tensely till the count of five; relax.

11. Point your left leg straight out, making tense muscles, count to five, then relax.

12. Do the same with your right leg. (Remember

to keep your eyes shut. Enjoy the total relaxation of your body muscles.)

13. Take five medium breaths.

Slowly breathe in through your nose and out through your mouth. As you breathe out through your mouth, think of the word "relax," and picture a tranquil scene. Be sure to let your entire body relax as you breathe.

Do the breathing exercises several times every day. And do the complete relaxation procedure at least once a day. You probably will not be able to do it all perfectly, or always regularly, every day. But the more regularly you do it, the more you will have peace, freedom from stomach pain, and *freedom* from outside pressures, including those from your alcoholic!

Please give this method a try, even though it takes effort, and you probably feel you have no more energy to spend on another thing you "have to do." The payoff will be tremendous. Do it just once, all the way through. See for yourself. You will feel less troubled, more detached from your alcoholic, less scared of him, and less anxious than you have felt in years. Keep it up. It is a lifesaver.

"Whatsoever things are true, whatsoever things are honest, whatsoever things are just, whatsoever things are pure, whatsoever things are lovely, whatsoever things are of good report; if there be any virtue; and if there be any praise, think on these things" (Phil. 4:8).

6
Don't Be Afraid of Losing Him Because You're Changing

You're not as dependent as you think you are.
Your alcoholic needs you more than (s)he will ever admit.
It's very hard to lose an alcoholic.

This chapter deals with what I call the "closet fear." If anyone were to ask me to name one thing that I believe stops most spouses of alcoholics from making changes in their relationships—changes they know will help—it's the fear that the alcoholic partner will leave.

I once heard it said most succinctly: "I was afraid of being rejected by a reject." Most of the audience winced when they heard that—they thought no one else had ever had that terrible thought. It seemed so dastardly to think of the alcoholic in those terms—but that's one of the most natural, normal feelings the spouse of the alcoholic has.

For years, you've been told by the alcoholic that

"you're the cause of it all," that you never do enough or do it right. You feel lower than a worm (except for the few times you feel like a saint). The alcoholic, on the other hand, is your tin god. *But not in society's eyes.* You know, and he knows, he is considered a reject. What could be worse than him leaving you, especially when you've invested all those years and expended your energy in an effort to help him?

And what do you get for it? He has you scared to death that he will leave you at the drop of a hat if you don't continue to do as he wants.

Now, most of the suggestions in this guide are deceptively simple; they seem "easy" to many people who do not live with an alcoholic, but any wife knows that as soon as she starts putting any of them into practice, her alcoholic will kick up a row.

Which brings us to an interesting point: who is really controlling your relationship? I'll bet you've been called the manager—the mommy. And the poor alcoholic is just shoved around by you, especially when he's feeling ashamed of past acts and slinks around the house, "taking abuse" from you.

But let's take a second look. Who is controlling whom—from behind-the-scenes? Who has whom revolving her life around him twenty-four hours a day? Who is thinking, worrying, stewing about him all the time? Neglecting your children, your hair, your mental condition, your intellectual improvement—everything? Who has you thinking that a million women "out there" are waiting for him? One alcoholic's wife, Miriam, has this to tell: "I left Joe for ten whole days—just to show him who needs whom. Do you know what? When I came home, he didn't even know I'd been gone!"

How do you deal with this?

First, you must remember two very important facts:

1. The alcoholic is an addict—a very dependent person. His dependence is not just on alcohol—he is very dependent on you. *He needs you.*

2. The alcoholic is a denier—he denies his alcoholism. He denies he is dependent on you. He says, instead, that you need him. He has you fooled into believing that you need him more than he needs you.

Knowing this—internalizing these truths—is very important, especially at the beginning of your recovery. It can give you the courage you need to start to make changes. I know the guilt you feel can keep you from changing: Are you thinking you are being "unfair" by "using" this knowledge of his dependency on you? Or are you saying to yourself, "He won't leave me if I make changes. *He* needs *me!*" GOOD! None of the changes you are going to make are unethical or vicious or wrong in any way. As a matter of fact, they are good for you, for the alcoholic and for the children. Understanding that your alcoholic needs you very much—and using this knowledge to help you get stronger—thereby helping him get well, is perfectly fine. After a while, when you are more able to, you will make changes just because they are good for you. But, right now, remember that he needs you and that you will probably not lose him—even though he may threaten it—as you grow.

What happens if you do lose him? Some alcoholics do storm out, calling your bluff, trying to scare you back into your place. Most come back, if you want them. But the way your relationship is now, you could probably replace your alcoholic with 1,000 others in one day by placing this ad in your Sunday newspaper: "Wanted: one mate; drunk 50 percent of the time; come and go as you please. Grateful family waits at home. All your housework done. Very few responsibilities expected to be met. You may interview family at your convenience to see if we meet your requirements."

You see, once you make these changes, you'll start to feel so good about yourself that you won't worry about him leaving you. You will like yourself so much that the "new you" will know she deserves a husband who respects her, likes her and treats her well. And when you begin to believe that and act like you believe it, your husband will treat you that way. I know it's difficult to believe that now; but trust me that it's true. I *know* it is—but you have to take a little step of faith and start making some changes— and then you'll see it's true.

God, help me to take my steps by faith and to keep on walking toward the wholeness you have for me.

7

Stop Arguing With Him
(It Works!)

It's like arguing with a bottle.
It's totally useless.

Often, when arguing with a drinking alcoholic, the argument is centered around trying to convince him that he's drinking, and that he's *denying,* again. This gets you furious, naturally. One wife, Sally, told me of the umpteen times she had confronted her husband with his drinking and his abusive behavior. He flatly denied he ever "did anything." Forgetting that "they deny," she got angry and argued with him about it—trying to convince him *and make him admit* that he was really drinking, or whatever it was that he was denying. *What got her so angry was that she began to realize that a tiny kernel of her inner being usually believed his denial nonsense, and thought, "There I go again, being crazy, misreading everything he does, like he says I do."*

Sally knew, deep down, that she did not have

illusions about his behavior. When she came into the therapy group, she really began to understand this. She learned that all the women living with alcoholics experienced the same denials—their husbands even used the same language, the same sentences to deny: "Yes, I admit I sometimes do—, but this time, I wasn't doing it" or "You always assume I do—; Don't you trust me?" or "It doesn't help me when you always accuse me."

The wives' answers were much the same also: "Why should I trust you? You've done it for five years. And already once today. Why shouldn't I suspect that you'll do it again, tonight?" Here is another typical reaction: "Maybe you weren't doing it this time, but you usually are." (The preceding one isn't said more than once or twice, usually, because it becomes cannon-fodder for the alcoholic to use in the future, an example to point to in an effort to "show" his wife that she's always "imagining it.") And when he says, "It doesn't help me when you accuse . . .," her defense often takes this form, "My 'accusing' you doesn't make you do it or not, because when I don't 'accuse,' you do it, anyway."

How can the wife stop this very exhausting merry-go-round? She must continually remind herself of these facts:

1. He probably really did it again.

2. If you must say something, say it only once and refuse to discuss it further. *Just be convinced of it*

yourself. In this way, he can't get to your vulnerability, your self-doubt about your sanity.

3. Keep telling yourself that he will continue to deny, deny, deny, as long as he is committed to staying sick. But remember that way down deep, he knows the truth, no matter what he says or how he rationalizes or twists his behavior when he tells it to a counselor, his mother, or whomever, to "prove" he was "unjustly attacked, again."

4. Remember that you have the right to leave him for any amount of time, to restore *your* sanity. It *is* tough to live with him.

As they say in the preamble to an Al-Anon meeting, "Living with an alcoholic is too much for most of us." These are comforting words. *You* are not a failure when it gets to be too much.

5. Keep telling yourself, after you've removed yourself from the room he's in, that you're not crazy. Remind yourself that he is very ill, that he will deny like he's always done, and that this denial or admission of guilt even, doesn't have much at all to do with whether or not he will "do it again." If he needs or wants to stay sick, he'll continue his behavior. If not, he will stop it. So tell yourself: "I won't worry whether he denies, admits, or whatever. What if he does admit that he did it again? Then, he will just promise, have some remorse for a while, and start all over. So, what's the difference?"

If, at this point, you are thinking, "I see all this, but . . .," it means your idea or motive still is to convince him you are right. Believe me, he knows that already. What you *must* start to believe is that you are right! *You are not crazy when you say you know he "did it again."*

Suppose once out of five times you do *imagine* that he hurt you—and he really didn't do anything? Consider what a wife of an alcoholic goes through, daily. She girds herself against the constant hurts she has *learned to expect.* So, if you are guilty of a "crime," it is not of attacking, or unjustly assuming—it is simply of flinching. And you want to stop flinching, not because it "accuses," "attacks," or any of that other *nonsense* the alcoholic accuses you of, but because it tears up your stomach, gives you constant attacks of nervousness and adds more chaos to your life.

Sally found this most helpful: When she has told herself the preceding facts and has finally convinced herself that she's not crazy, she then goes off to where he isn't—into the bathroom, bedroom, spare room or backyard. She then picks up a favorite book and reads to restore her mind, and refresh herself. Inside of five minutes she's feeling 100 times better.

Quickly get out this chapter the next time these things happen. Really think about these ideas. Try very hard to believe in yourself. It will start to work for you. Do this each time it happens. Some of you will see results the first time. For others, it will take a while, depending on how strong the alcoholic's hold is on you in this area. If this is a particularly difficult area, do not despair. Just keep working at it. And it will work for you.

Help me to increase my capacity for enjoying the little pleasures of life daily. Keep me calm in the midst of life's storms.

8
Do One Thing Every Day Just for Yourself

Make it last for at least fifteen minutes.
It must be something that is pure fun.
It must be something that is just for you.

This does not mean housework, cooking or cleaning—even if you are a gourmet cook, a terrific baker, or derive great pleasure from seeing a clean house and sparkling floors.

Spouses of alcoholics find all kinds of ways to continue their role of "always taking care of others." If their husbands like pies, they turn into bake fiends. If their spouses demand a crazy-clean house, "just like his mother always had," they *love* to clean. If the alcoholic demands that the wife be thrifty (and they always do; pay no attention to bar bills, though), then she learns to sew and make everything, even the family's winter coats!

"So what's wrong with all that?" you ask. "What's wrong with being a good wife?"

Plenty. We are not discussing the idea of being a good wife—you crossed that line a long time ago. We are discussing the situation that's turning you from a good wife into a milksop, martyr, and slave to your situation.

I know very few spouses of alcoholics who have not found themselves in this snare. It applies to even those who are resentful and don't "keep up" the house—they may live in rags themselves. They don't fix their hair, buy almost no new clothes, and let their looks deteriorate. *It seems that if you are good to yourself in any one area—and that means doing what you want, not what the alcoholic wants you to do—you make yourself feel guilty and pay for it by punishing yourself another way.*

You do not deserve to be punished for being nice to yourself. Remember, you did not cause the drinking. The alcoholic is past master at being able to make you feel guilty. That is why you have been punishing yourself.

Some of you are going to say, "Oh, he has no control over me; I don't think I punish myself." *When was the last time you were good to yourself on a regular basis?* Do you go to movies, plays, museums, buy yourself fresh flowers, get yourself a present without buying something for someone else first? Do you get yourself a babysitter so that you can go out with your friends?

"But I don't have any time."

"But I don't have any money."

"But I don't have any energy."

No energy? That could be depression—anger turned inward. No wonder you're angry. For years, it's been all work, turmoil and no play. Anyone would be depressed. Do you know what they do in mental hospitals when someone is very depressed? They take that patient to the gymnasium and let her bat a ball around—for fun—to help her get out that anger. No use keeping it in; it's just tearing up your stomach. So, if you are very depressed—sleep a lot or can't sleep; eat too much, or can't eat; sigh a lot—*get your muscles moving*. Make one of the things you do for fun every day something physical. *But make it something you enjoy. Don't add any more "shoulds" to your life. Part of your resentment and depression is that you take on too many responsibilities you really don't enjoy—too many "shoulds."* Think of what you'd *like* to do. Do something different, something exotic. Take up a sport that uses a lot of arm muscles—where you have to hit a ball hard, or jump rope—learn to be a gymnast! Get books from the library on European and South American sports—do something special. Something just for you.

"But I thought you've got to *talk* away depression. And once you have gotten to the *core* of things, your anger will just melt." (Heard that before?) On the contrary, many therapists now agree that you can *act your way to right feelings*. In other words, act as if you are not depressed. Hold your chin up. (It's hard to stay depressed when you walk that way.) Do all the things you would do if you were feeling cheerful. But also cry when you need to. Unmask your feelings and deal with them. But when your cry is over, keep on going. Let yourself feel your feelings—but just *accept* them and *don't attach very much importance to them*. (They're very fickle, you know.)

Your depression will pass. All bad feelings pass when you begin to accept them. And accept that it will take time to adjust yourself to your new attitude!

Let's get back to your excuses about why you aren't doing nice things for yourself. No money? That one's easy. Do free things. Look in the Sunday paper. Call the local universities, museums, libraries. They have public relations departments. Get on their mailing lists for things to do. Go to parks, free films, lectures, concerts, fashion shows, gallery openings. Browse in bookstores, window-shop, sit by a brook, lie back and listen to the stereo.

No time to do anything? Everyone has fifteen minutes a day to use in a way he pleases. The amount of time is not as important as the fact that you will be doing something fun for yourself on a *regular* basis.

What kinds of results can you expect from this? It may seem strange to hear this, but at first you may feel uncomfortable, guilty. This is your "old" self, trying, unconsciously, to trick you into staying down. *Do not pay attention to it.* It is like a child having a tantrum. Sure, it feels "bad" to make changes—but it also feels bad to stay in the same, rotten mess you've been in! *If you are going to feel bad whether or not you change, you might as well use that pain to grow instead of staying upset. If you don't grow, the pain will not ease. If you choose to grow, the pain will go away.*

The first time Margie bought herself a gift—not for her husband, not for her kids—she felt extremely guilty. But she thought, "Love thy neighbor as thyself"—not *more than* thyself. And spouses of alcoholics have for so long been on the end of the spectrum of giving, giving, giving, that they feel very selfish when they start to give to themselves. It seems cruel, wrong. And you might feel that way at first, because you are not used to doing these things for yourself.

Being good to yourself is a very important part of your recovery from the effects of alcoholism. And when *you* start to change, and recover, your whole family will start to get well.

God, give me grace to see myself as you see me and treat myself as you treat me.

9
Use Tough Love

Tough love is tough on everybody.
It hurts as much as surgery.
And it's every bit as necessary.

Guilt.

Spouses of alcoholics are known for their inability to be able to see their alcoholic partners suffer. Seldom can the wife of an alcoholic stand to see her husband suffer *alone*. She must suffer *with* him, or she feels guilty.

Rescuing.

If you are going to do all you can to help your alcoholic recover—and that means preventing him from dying or going irretrievably insane—then you must learn to stop "helping" him. You must learn to stop rescuing the alcoholic. Learn how to stop believing, "But he's suffering so much! I *must* help him!" Because if you continue to "help" your alcoholic, you will be helping to keep him sick.

Tender, loving care?

Fine for other diseases. Alcoholism is such a crazy disease, if you help your alcoholic in the same way you would help a loved one with cancer, heart disease, or tuberculosis—you'll be helping him to drown in his own blood.

Forgive yourself.

Okay. So you rescued him before; you did it for years. You didn't know better. Forgive yourself and keep on going. (Remember, you didn't cause this disease!)

What is tough love?

If your two-year-old goes in the street, continually, after repeated warnings—you apply a little wisdom to his bottom. What's his reaction? He screams; he is mortified; he looks terrible; he tries to make you feel guilty. But you do it anyway, to save his life. And sometimes you still feel rotten.

That's something like how tough love feels when you start doing it, with your alcoholic.

It's letting him hurt enough to want to get well.

It means letting all his crises happen to him without erasing the painful consequences for him any more. It means that when he's hurting very badly, you don't raise a finger to help—otherwise, he won't have the incentive to reach for *real* help. The crisis you didn't allow to happen may have been the one he

41

needed to make him reach for the phone and call A.A.

He'll never make that phone call for help if he doesn't hurt. *No alcoholic ever woke up one fine morning and stretched and smiled and said, "I think I'll get sober today!"*

People don't seek help if they don't hurt.

I can't stand to see him hurt!

You may say, "But I'm the kind of person who just *can't* stand by and watch him hurt. After all, you said it's a disease. And he's so physically sick from it already. He's so weak. He can't do for himself. He's so pitiful!"

I know how tough it is on you.

But going through the painful consequences of his disease for him—or erasing them for him—will just postpone the day when he will get the real help that will keep him alive.

And—I know this is harsh—you're probably doing the rescuing not for your alcoholic, but because of your own feelings of guilt and your fear of losing the alcoholic—your fear that he might leave and find himself another rescuer.

Think about that.

What's more important? Your feelings? Or his dying? You can learn to deal with your feelings. Go to Al-Anon; see a counselor. But, do the things you must do, if you want to help him live. It's urgent.

42

Let him have dignity.

Tough love means letting go—truly and completely, of his disease. It means minding your own business. It means letting him have the dignity to pick up the pieces of his life and not be an emotional cripple, any more.

What else?

Tough love means not pouring out the booze, not filling the bottles with water, not marking them. It means not looking for bottles, not paying any attention to them. It means not buying him booze. It means not driving him home from the hospital when he asks you for help. It means leaving him there, not driving him *away* from his help. It means making all the changes suggested in this book.

So why is this still so hard for you?

Why do these words still sound so cruel and heartless to you? *Because you've been bluffed by your alcoholic's disease for so long that you think he is asking for help when it's really the disease that is asking you to help. Don't rescue that disease any longer.*

He's not too sick to recover.

If you think "this won't work" for *your* alcoholic, maybe you think he's beyond any help. This isn't true. He has an 80 percent better chance to recover if you practice tough love!

Act as if you can do it.

You don't have to *feel* differently in order to *act* differently. And don't worry—acting with tough love won't make you into a tough, unfeeling person. It will just make you very much like a doctor: a person who performs necessary surgery in order to save a life—even if it hurts.

You're not mean.

A priest, well-known in the field of alcoholism, told a group of wives that "if you think you've 'sinned' it is in the area of babying him too much— rather than what you think, that you're too 'mean.'"

Do it for him.

If all else fails—if you can't stop feeling guilty— *do it for him*. That's what tough love is all about.

Spare me from sympathy and self-pity by helping me to see reality as it is; help me, God, to see my life and my relationships more objectively.

10
Don't Ride With Him
When He's Drunk

*Don't put up with his "cute" games of gunning the
motor, driving too fast, letting go of the wheel
(and holding it with his knees).*

*Don't be afraid of losing him to someone else if
you say "no" to this kind of driving.*

*He won't drive more or less carefully, whether
you're with him or not. Remember this when you
worry about whether he will hurt himself.*

Ever heard of the Serenity Prayer? One doesn't
have to be religious to try its principles for living: the
serenity to accept the things we cannot change; the
courage to change the things we can; and the wisdom
to know the difference.

What's involved in the case of a drunken driver?
He's already been drinking, and it's a snowballing
thing. *He needs more booze.* And there's nothing
you can do, now, about that. It would be like trying
to change the chemistry of a diabetic's blood. Since

he has already taken the first drink, all the pleading, threatening, yelling, and crying in the world, won't stop his need; it's even too great for him. Staying or getting in the car won't stop him from needing those other drinks. A person trying to stop a disease-need is like a grain of sand trying to stop an oak tree from growing. So, save yourself. And if you have children, do not allow them to drive with him when he's been drinking. Just one or two drinks has sufficiently decreased his reaction time so that he could kill himself, you, the children, and other children who unexpectedly run into the street. If he's going to do it, don't let your children go along, no matter what he says. If you have no money to send them to where they're going, unless it's a matter of life or death, they can stay home. If you have to go to work, and they have to go to the babysitter's, find a closer babysitter. *Don't set them up to drive with their father when he's drinking. This is one place where you must draw the line.* This is a life-and-death situation for everyone.

Your alcoholic may tell you: (1) "A couple of drinks increases my driving skills, makes me more sharp;" (2) "You always make a big deal out of nothing;" (3) "Where's your sense of humor?"; (4) "I'll be careful, I promise;" or (5) "You're turning the children against their own father!" All these statements are to be expected from alcoholics who are drinking and driving and who want to deny how serious it is. If he didn't talk in such an out-of-touch-with-reality manner much of the time, he wouldn't be an alcoholic. So, expect that talk. Ignore it, and do what you need to in order to protect yourself and the children.

You do not have to explain to him what you are doing or why you are doing it. Be as calm as possible; just say *no* when he says, "Get in the car." If you feel a temptation to argue, get out of the room and don't listen to him. Alcoholics go on and on when they're drinking and they want to "prove" a point.

Just do what you need to do for safety's sake. He won't remember much anyway.

You can't protect him from the world twenty-four hours a day. You'll drop from exhaustion if you try.

This is hard to do, but once you've let him go without you in the car, try not to worry. There's nothing you can do about the situation, whether you're in the car or not. Now that you're not in the dangerous situation, why punish yourself for saving your life *as you should*, and sit and feel guilty all day?

If you had been in the car, and an accident had occurred, you couldn't have done anything but gotten hurt anyway.

Try to see this situation objectively. If you were your best friend, would you tell yourself that it was wrong to feel guilty for not getting hurt along with him?

It doesn't help to worry. You can do nothing to

prevent him from getting sicker—that's the nature of his progressive disease. You don't have to—*you aren't supposed to*—get sicker with him. *Get well yourself. Try to become emotionally detached from his disease. When you have a choice, and you do in this case, you are supposed to remove yourself from the source of infection in order to avoid the effects of a disease.* Pretend your alcoholic is emotionally quarantined. If he is, you are free to go about your life in a healthy, adult, reasonable, content frame of mind. He can drive, drink, whatever he wants to do, if he chooses to stay sick. But you have a duty to yourself not to get sick with worry and guilt along with him.

Anything that means "letting go" of his disease by you, helps him move closer to sobriety, if he should choose it.

It may not seem like it at the time (and it probably won't) but you are not "mean" or "uncaring" when you save yourself and your children from the consequences of his alcoholism. If you do this, you help save him from *more guilt*. You free him to make a choice of whether to get sober or not.

Remember, the first few times you do the things suggested in this book, they will feel strange, even "wrong." That is a natural reaction, when you've been stuck in old, sick habit patterns. But those are *just feelings*. Pay no attention to them. Your long-range goal is health for yourself, your children, your husband. If you do the right things, no matter how odd they seem to you, you are helping everyone get well.

Help me, God, to make the right choices.

11

Confront Him!

Confront him when he's sober.
Confront him when you're calm.

There are all kinds of confrontations.

You've probably been yelling, crying, threatening and giving the silent treatment for years. Those kinds of confrontations are ineffective. Sure, they let off steam, for a while. But the anger and frustration and depression return, maybe even stronger.

So what kind of confrontation works with an alcoholic?

1. Don't do anything while he's drunk. Wait till morning.

2. Say what is necessary only once. State it calmly and refuse to discuss, debate or defend what you say. Don't listen to explanations or excuses. Simply state facts.

3. Don't do this when you're angry. In order not to get into an argument, leave the room or house for a while.

4. Tell him what he does when he drinks. (See the chapter on blackouts.) Tell him the effects his drinking has on you, the kids, his family and yours, and his career. Tell him he needs help. Tell him you believe he has a disease called alcoholism.

5. Tell him you're not ashamed of him—that you know he has a disease. Insist that he get help. You want a *live* husband.

6. Read about this disease. Tell him about the 144 secondary diseases related to alcoholism. Tell him that alcoholism is fatal and that you will no longer believe his denials.

7. Don't repeat this process more than once.

8. He may very well deny, later, that you said what you did, or he may tell you that you are full of baloney. *Don't react to this bluff. He's scared to death. Good. He should be.*

9. Confront him with his disease as often as you can. How?

   A. Leave A.A. literature in the bathroom, after you've removed the other magazines. A great pamphlet is "Brain Damage Starts With the First Drink." Get the literature by writing to Narcotics Education, Inc. [Box 4390/Tacoma Park, Maryland 20912] and asking them to send it to you. It's free. Don't respond to your husband's yelling or sarcastic comments. Do it just once. Don't ask him if he's read it. He will.

   B. Each time you don't rescue him from the painful consequences of his drinking, *you are allowing him to be confronted by his disease.* That is the best thing you can do to help him get closer to sobriety.

Genuineness and honesty are godly qualities. Let these become a real part of my life.

12
Walk Away From Abuse

The battering will get worse.
It won't just stop "tomorrow."
Things are as bad as you think.
Not being battered is certainly a reasonable expectation from a husband!

Denial is the name of the game in alcoholism.

The family also denies. They deny that it's as bad as it is. They may say *"But,* it will get better tomorrow," or *"But,* I'm probably overreacting. It's not as bad as I thought it was," or *"But*, he's so wonderful when he's not hurting me. We're so close—closer than other couples. Oh, when he's good, he's very, very good—and when he's bad, he's horrid." All these denial sentences. They get repeated, thousands of times over, in alcoholic homes every day by terrified wives, by wives who don't want it to be so bad.

Articles tell you to "accept" your mate as he is with all his "little character defects." Well, that may be just fine for "regular" families, but for wives of alcoholics, that can be damaging advice, if taken the wrong way. *Acceptance doesn't mean accepting unacceptable behavior—it means accepting the reality of a situation as it is, and then dealing with it in a sane, life-preserving manner.* It means you *must* stop believing fairy tales. Alcoholism and its side effects don't get prayed away and they don't get wished away. The abuse caused by the alcoholic— whether it's physical or mental—isn't prevented by pleading, crying, threatening, explaining, analyzing, having good intentions, making promises, or punctuating sullen silences with temper tantrums. *And if you don't do something to stop the abuse—no one will, because the alcoholic doesn't have the motivation you have. He has the need for power.*

And, in a sick way, it's "fun" for him (like the neighborhood bully). *You're* the one getting beaten up physically and/or emotionally. If you want it to stop, then follow these steps. You must learn this new way of living without being hurt. Statistics show that abused wives choose abusing husbands over and over again, if *they* don't change their way of relating to men.

Use these ideas, whether you stay with your alcoholic or not. If you stay with him, it will have a definite effect: *you* will no longer be the person you were, expecting to be hurt. You will learn not to tolerate it, not to expect it, not to want it. Your husband will either change enough in the process to come along with you and get well, or he won't. But you won't have lost. If he doesn't change? Then you will be a beaten wife no longer. It's that simple. This may horrify you. You may exclaim, "Oh, no, I don't want to give him up!" *Think* about what you are saying. Do you really want him if the condition for keeping him is that you must agree to be beaten up for the next twenty years?

It *is* very hard to admit to this reality. To admit that your husband is sick enough to regularly hurt you physically and/or emotionally is extremely difficult indeed. But it is probably even more depressing when you think about the abuse to your self-image that comes from taking his mistreatment. It probably even horrifies you to think "you're that kind of woman" who expects no more than to be treated like dirt. Your family, your friends, and maybe even your therapist pity you, don't understand you, and cannot see why you keep "going back for more."

They don't know the "hooking" lines he gives you that make you feel like a "good woman" (like when he says "you're so good" or "thank you so much for sticking with me through this stuff while I try to get well"). In your healthier moments, you feel like a patsy, not a saint, when he says this. You wince, instead of glowing.

But be careful about your anger. You probably find yourself getting so enraged at your collusion with him in the deception that you're "so good" to take all that stuff, you often just explode, feel guilty afterwards for "punishing" him "back," then feel sorry for him. And then you don't make a move to change your situation, *because of your guilt*.

That's why you must learn to constructively channel your anger into healthy action for you that doesn't bring on unnecessary guilt. It must be action that moves you to a higher plane of living: *that of just not taking it any more*. Because yelling and screaming and the accompanying guilt are just cop-outs for not taking the risk to change your situation.

What have you got to lose? *Another* five, ten, or more years of being hurt over and over? Stop falling for the old con job that you're losing a prince of a guy when you say no to abuse. If he's really a prince, he will want you even more when you act like the princess instead of a doormat. *A truly good husband doesn't get angry at this wife for not wanting to be beaten up.*

Another important thing to remember: If you are depressed, ashamed, despairing about all this—*try to remember that it's basically not your problem!* You're only depressed because you feel trapped, because you've been trained through years of living with alcoholism to believe his problems were yours to bear. *Once you learn how to say no to abuse, there is no longer any part of this problem that's yours.* That's a cause to feel happy for yourself; *and you do have that right, you know.* You don't have to feel guilty for not feeling bad *with* your husband—not suffering *with* him for *his* problem.

But let's look at that. Is he really suffering? His self-centered system is so strong that he doesn't feel sorry for *you*—he feels sorry for *him*. He feels sorry that you "abandoned" *him*. (When you learn to say no to abuse he sees it as you abandoning him.)

Sure, he's sick. But feeling sorry for an alcoholic *never* got him well. *Get yourself well and feel happy for you. That is the best medicine you can bring into your household. It can help set the stage for everyone—you, your kids, and your husband—to all get well.*

What do you do when he physically hits you or mentally abuses you?

DON'T:

1. Stay up all night trying to "show him" how he went wrong.

2. Try to convince him that you didn't provoke it—that he *really* is wrong.

3. Assume that you caused it.

4. Think you probably bring out "the beast" in him.

5. Feel sorry for him.

6. Explain or discuss anything.

7. Think he doesn't know what he did.

DO:

1. Remove yourself physically from his fists.

2. Tell yourself it is a very bad situation.

3. Leave immediately when he hits—or if it's mental cruelty, leave or tell him to leave that minute.

4. Stay away from him for a few days, with no mention of where you are. *Let him worry.*

5. When you return, or let him come back, do not discuss what happened. Do not believe his denial, his confused "I really don't know what happened to make you act like this!" *He knows.*

6. If and when it happens again, leave, or ask him to leave *immediately,* with no discussion. Don't get back together as quickly as before and no discussion about the episode when you get together again.

7. Understand that he'll get the message: *You will no longer tolerate abuse.*

MORE TIPS:

1. Be gentle with yourself. If you cannot do it all at once, or even for a while, that's okay. *But store it on a. shelf, knowing you can do this later.* This method works for many people. What it will do is help transform you into a person who is self-respecting, *who will not be abused, any more.*

2. This method will free your husband to choose to get well—free him to learn how to treat you without abusing you. The old saying, "You've got to be willing to lose, in order to win," applies here. You've got to want to be self-respecting so much that you are willing to lose your marriage, if necessary, to get that. If your husband is a hard-core abuser of many years, it is often only this "drastic" action that

can force him to face squarely the seriousness of his disease. Free yourself. Then, he will be free to choose health too, if he wants it. This is probably the first time in his life that anyone has cared as much as you do—in the right way.

3. This approach is difficult but it is a way out of the trap you think you are in.

A soft answer turneth away wrath.

13
Accept Yourself

Accept the fact that you can't leave emotionally.
Accept the realization that you hate staying.
Both of these feelings are normal.

Your mind is probably so panicked and befuddled by now that you really can't make a rational decision.

Things have probably come to another crisis point. You may be depressed most of the time or panicky and anxious most of the time or your feelings about your husband may fluctuate considerably. You hate him when he hurts you—and you feel sorry for him when he cries afterwards, in his typical childlike way, because he is truly sorry for what he did, and horrified at his own inability to stop himself. Your pity isn't just maudlin; you realize he really means it when he says he feels terrible about his actions. You feel his pain *with* him. And then, when he turns around and does it again, you feel so enraged, so betrayed, that it causes your head to spin.

You cannot believe that any sane human being would keep doing this kind of thing over and over.

You're right. No sane person would. But your husband isn't sane. When he's not being treated for his disease, it runs rampant—and overpowers any will-power your husband could use. And all the very hurtful things that happen to you and the kids because of it will continue to happen until his disease is treated. In fact, it will get worse, if it goes on being untreated. Your husband needs *help*—and he's probably too panic-stricken to get it without outside persuasion. That persuasion often comes in the form of his wife appearing to be the "mean one" by insisting that he get help and *stay* in treatment. Otherwise, she will walk out and stay out until he agrees to get treatment—or just walk out and stay out—period!

Okay, you'd like to be at that point, but you're not. You feel you cannot do this any more than he can go willingly for help. But that won't last forever. You just can't do it this minute, this hour, this day. Remember, alcoholism is a *family* disease, and everybody has terrible fears, panics. Everybody feels like a baby who should be taken care of. No one can take care of anyone else. Everyone is resentful that people are leaning on them. What *is* right is that everybody in that house needs help; what is wrong is that everybody is looking to the wrong people for help—the other people in that helpless household! We all desperately want our husbands and wives to be parents to us at times, but in the alcoholic home, it gets to the point where no adult *can* act like an adult and no adult *wants* to be an adult. Everybody wants everyone else to be a protective person. And all the wishing, hating and resenting in the world isn't going to change the reality of that very terrible, deep sickness in everyone. As my mother used to say, "You may not like it—but what are you going to do? Beat your head against a brick wall?" How many years have you been beating your head against that brick wall? He's not going to be a responsible, kind, husband—without long and sustained treatment— because he can't be.

Many people get angry and resentful at a sick person when he gets sick and can no longer perform his functions and roles in the family. I treated a woman whose husband sustained irreversible brain damage. They can no longer be the fashioned, stylized, "marvelous couple" people used to think they were. The wife is still very angry and very disappointed in her husband. She also feels very guilty for her anger—since she knows he is very ill. This has lasted five years now, and the wife has made almost no adjustment to the reality of her situation. She's just more bitter, more entrenched in her loneliness. She has cut herself off from all her former friends, and is less willing to make necessary changes in her life style to ensure that she doesn't go down the drain too.

It's very human to be panicked and furious and depressed by the reality of your husband's alcoholism, but you must try to clear your mind and remember these points:

1. The fears that keep you from leaving him are terrible and very real. You do understand that he needs an incentive to get sober: losing you. But you're afraid, way down deep, that (a) you can't manage emotionally or financially without him; (b) he will find another woman; (c) he will like being alone, with no one to answer to, no one to be responsible for, no kids to look after; (d) *you* will like his absence (the absence of pain) and not even want him back and the guilt from that thought is almost unbearable; (e) he will play a big "game" about this whole thing and instead of seeing this separation time as a time to get treatment, he will punish you and threaten you that he will die, hurt you or never come back; or (f) all or any of the above.

It is very important for you to understand that the alcoholic is more dependent on you than you are on him, *although both of you live under the illusion that it's the other way around.* When you realize this truth you'll be able to take measures to get help for you and your kids. And you don't have to let go of your fears before you take action. Take action—and then the fears will drop! It's an act of faith. You have to get the courage to take that first step, in blind faith that it will all work out.

2. If he goes on being untreated, he will get sicker, more cruel, more mean, less kind, less responsible— those characteristics are part and parcel of this

63

progressive disease called alcoholism. Alcoholism doesn't get better by just praying, by standing still and hoping it will go away. You have to take action. You must *do* something. And if you do something to get help, that action will affect the alcoholic in a positive way. No family member can remain unaffected by another family member getting help and getting better.

3. You may have to hurt some more before you can take a step to get out of the mess you find yourself in. If you are as panicked, as inert, as immobilized, as many women are then you may have to wait awhile till you finally can say to yourself (without guilt getting too much in the way): "I *do* deserve to be able to escape this mess!" Then, maybe you can take measures to find help for housing, and finances, and emotional help, for you and your children to get out—or try to have your husband sent into treatment, even if he won't go willingly.

4. There are many support systems open to you; the mistake many women make is that they only go to one. They may avail themselves of a place that helps them get a job or a loan, or go to a place where there is emotional support, but they fail to find good, solid financial advice. Try all the services that are available to you (and don't let pride stand in the way). Call Displaced Homemakers; call a crisis line and ask for the number of the Battered Wives' Center—they will often set up counseling to help you get a job and a temporary home. Go to a free treatment center or a

sliding-scale clinic and get personal counseling. And very important: this is a good time to get yourself to Al-Anon and to take your kids to Al-Ateen. These organizations are for family members of alcoholics. *All* the people in the meetings know exactly what you're going through—because they've been there themselves. It's *free;* there's usually a meeting nightly, and sometimes during the day. Ask the telephone operator for the number. If there's no listing, call Alcoholics Anonymous and ask them for the nearest Al-Anon meeting place. One of the best things they will offer you is a twenty-four-hour network of support. When you go to a meeting, you can ask for the phone numbers of members who are willing to have you call them anytime. They understand the daily and hourly fears and crises that occur. This service is completely anonymous—you only have to give your first name. If you don't have a car, call the Al-Anon answering service and they will often get another woman to pick you up and bring you home from meetings. It is very important for you to stay in treatment (preferably Al-Anon) during separation from your husband or during his hospitalization. This will help to keep your hopes up and your guilt down.

5. You *can* get him out of the house—if he's threatening you or himself. Often the police won't arrest him. (They will say it's a "family squabble" and are reluctant to arrest alcoholics, because wives frequently will bail out their husbands the next

morning anyway.) You can go to the Supreme Bench's Court-system's Medical Division and get him picked up for a psychiatric evaluation. You should explain that you want him committed to an alcoholism treatment center. If you do have him arrested—*don't bail him out.* Instead, go to the judge at the hearing and ask that your husband be sent into treatment for his disease instead of to jail. The judge will often respect a wife's wish in this. Find a mental health counselor who understands this route, and who will go with you and support you throughout the hearing. The judge will be more amenable to getting your husband into treatment when he knows you are serious about getting help for yourself.

6. Understand that he can't get well overnight. Often, he will beg you to come back, or for you to allow him to come home—too early. Be careful at this point. Decide to see him or not see him according to your ability to handle being around him while he's so newly sober. It takes *time* for him to learn how to treat his family nicely. Long years of habit don't go away overnight. If you take him back and find he's unbearable, you not only have the right—but the duty to yourself and your sanity—to say, "It's too soon." You can be loving about it. He may try to make you feel guilty, but that's only because he's scared and angry and *he's too sick, maybe, at that point, to make a rational decision*—so you may have to be the one to say, "Not yet." Give

yourselves—both of you—time enough to become whole people before you get back together. That way, your marriage will have a chance.

Help me in my struggle to accept myself and to realize that my feelings are normal.

14

Don't Believe "Drunk Is Fun!"

He's absolutely crazy if he acts like it's fun.
Living with him is like living in an insane asylum—
without doctors.
No one in the "outside world" who is not an
alcoholic thinks his world is fun—or sane!

Carol sat in my office with her brow wrinkled, trying to believe me.

I repeated, "He's *not* having fun out there!"

"But you've been telling me that for weeks and he comes in all puffed up and smug and gives me that horrible grin—like he has the world all wrapped up just the way he wants it and like he has such contempt for me!" She was crying. The anguish had been going on for so long, and there didn't seem to be any hope that it would change.

Carol went on, "I know you told me not to talk to Ted about what we talk about, just to *do* the changes, but I got so mad at him. I yelled at him last week, right after my therapy session. I told him I *knew* he wasn't having any fun. And I thought that would stop him from trying to hurt me with the idea that he goes out there where all the women want him, in those bars.

"But I was really thrown by what he said. I got *so* angry! He just outsmarted me again! He acted like he knew what I was going to say and he knew just what to say to hook me into being afraid again.

"He became real serious-looking, like he was the sober one and I was the drunk. And then he started talking to me in that tone of voice I hate—like he's a social worker. He sure can pull that one off when he's drunk—and get me to react just as I would if I didn't know he was drunk!

"He told me, 'That's right, honey. I'm *not* having fun out there. What ever made you think otherwise? I've got a disease! And that's why you'll have to be patient!' And then he just grinned at me.

"I could have killed him!"

Not every alcoholic is like Carol's husband. He has a college degree and was a counselor at a halfway house for adolescent boys before his drinking grew worse. But there's one thing he does have in common with a lot of alcoholics: a knowledge of manipulation skills.

Let's take a look at the dynamics of that discussion between Carol and Ted. Let's see what *really* happened. Ted accomplished several things in one fell swoop:

1. He used his "social worker voice" on her, knowing it hooked into her feelings of inferiority about her own sanity.

2. He succeeded in making her temporarily forget that *he* is sick. Carol didn't fall for this again though. She kept this analogy in mind when he tried to pull it off again: I asked her to think this way whenever he would try the I'm-the-doctor-and-you're-the-patient routine again: "Think, imagine, that he is where he belongs—in the hospital, getting treatment for his very sick condition—his physical and mental illness. Then, you visit him. You've been peaceful for a few days, because he is away from the house. You walk into the room *and he pretends he's a gracious host and you're the patient,* about to be admitted to the back wards of a mental hospital. *But he has the pajamas on!*

"Imagine the look on the *real* doctor's face when he happens to walk in the room at that time, seeing and hearing all this. The doctor confronts your husband with the reality that *he's* the patient and *you* are the visitor."

The next time her husband tried to make her feel crazy, Carol tried this. She "tuned him out," kept her mouth shut, and became very thoughtful. She thought about this imaginary scene of her husband being where he belonged: in the hospital. Then she looked at him very differently. She was shocked and horrified by his irrational behavior, but detached from it too.

And he saw her detachment.

But more importantly, Carol *felt* that detachment. *That was the first time Carol was able to give his disease back to him, where it belonged.*

Your husband probably uses the same kind of technique to make you blow up. Your husband may not succeed at making you think he's a doctor and you're a patient, but he probably does make you think you're a bad mother or too religious or a lousy housekeeper. What's *his* way of "getting to you"?

If your husband and Ted changed places for three weeks, Ted would find a way to make you explode with anger and/or fear, just the way your husband does now. Likewise, your husband would "get to" Carol. That's one of the horrible ways the disease of alcoholism works. When the alcoholic is still sick, he always does this to his wife.

After that happened with Ted, he went out again that night, played his "games," and came in looking like he had had a good time. This happened in spite of the fact that he had just told her the day before, "It is true—I'm not having any fun. How could I? I have a disease."

What's really going on here?

Sure, Ted goes out to "have fun." But it's with hate and resentment and fear in his heart. He knows, *no matter how much he denies it,* that it's not at all as innocent as he says it is. No matter *how* much

"Charlie down the street" says, "Ted isn't doing anything wrong." (That's one of the excuses Ted always gives Carol.)

But, *is* he having fun?

Ted is charming. But so are most alcoholics.

Ted is attractive. He has a way with words. Most alcoholics know how to make a surface connection rather quickly with people, especially with those members of the opposite sex who "hook" easily into their games.

But what happens after that? What happens when Ted begins talking? He attacks; he puts his wife down; he manipulates.

He thinks he has such great friends. And they're all as sick as he is, down at the bar—his drinking buddies. They make hearty promises to each other—break them and forget them. They have contempt for each other and for themselves.

Ted gets deeper into his sickness with every encounter he chooses to make in that bar atmosphere.

Do other women "have" him? *Nobody "has" Ted—except his sickness. That's what "has" Ted.*

Ted is too wrapped up in his fears, resentments, and hates to relate at all, in *any* appropriate way, for more than a short time, to anyone.

But Ted's denial system doesn't just mean he denies his drinking. He needs to deny—because he is very, very ill—that these other behaviors are sick. He needs to pretend to himself and his wife *and others*—that he is *in control.*

So, if Ted's not having fun, and if Carol is detached, she doesn't have to put up with his behavior.

If Carol is going to get her perspective back—*if she's going to stop "hooking" into his disease*—she's got to get away from his disease. She has to give his disease back to him. And that means *he,* not *she,* will then start getting the painful consequences of his actions.

So, how does Carol do this? Some people can become detached, if their alcoholics aren't as cruel as Carol's, while staying with them, and not leaving them.

Other people find that living with someone who tries to emotionally threaten them ten times in one day is too much to live with. In such a situation, one must keep a guard up for so long that it's like living a lion tamer's existence.

Every woman has to find the right way for her to get out from under *his* disease. Read this book. Try using the ideas in it. Talk to a counselor. Reason things out. But remember: *You do not have to be trapped.*

God is faithful. He will not allow you to be tested above your capacities, but he will make a way to escape for you.

15

Tell Your Families?
Only If *You* Want To!

Both sets of parents are adults.
He does have a disease.
You are not a failure because your husband got sick.

This is yet another problem that needs to be dealt with—how to handle the feelings of his parents and yours. Would they blame you—or feel you were a failure—if he contracted diabetes? People don't often act rationally when it comes to alcoholism; but now that you have the facts, *you* can be rational and hope they will understand.

Here are the facts to keep in mind:

1. You don't owe the world an explanation.

2. You are an adult. You don't have to tell mommy or daddy everything any more.

3. If you're *sure* you're going to get a lot of flak about it—why tell them? Forget it, unless, of course, you want to stew about it, and become exhausted

and mad at yourself.

Drop the guilt feelings. Get into doing something enjoyable. If you do, you'll forget about your guilt, and when you do remember your worry, you'll be so refreshed, you'll be able to think about it rationally and *finalize* your decision.

Remember also that your decision whether to tell the parents is *just a choice, not an important life decision. Don't exaggerate its importance.* (In the alcoholic home, *so* much seems *so* important all the time. Everything is magnified out of proportion.) If it's not necessary to tell the parents, if it will just hurt them, if it will just have repercussions on *you,* then do the sensible thing and for everyone's sake, drop it.

Give me the wisdom to be sensible in my decision making.

16

Mean What You Say and Say What You Mean

Think before you make a threat or a promise.
You can conquer your guilt feelings.
Learn to accept yourself as a human being.

One of my clients, Caroline, recently wore an outfit that seemed to blend with the décor of my office. She was wearing a Mexican poncho over a loosely fitting dress, and knee socks with sandals. Near her, on the wall next to bamboo roll-up shades, is my favorite Diego Rivera print, framed in heavy fruitwood. But Caroline's words did not coincide with her appearance. She sounded scared, small, and was lacking in self-confidence. Her husband, Josh, had just outmaneuvered her so well that her head was still spinning when she walked in.

"I decided to try to get courageous and follow through on your suggestion to just ask him to leave when he got nasty, instead of explaining and discussing," she started.

Caroline and Josh are separated. He visits her from time to time, when she can handle it. Someday soon I hope she will be able to go beyond simply "handling it" to creatively deciding what she wants from life. Then she will go after her goals—to be content, peaceful—instead of just getting through her husband's sickness and coping with cruelty.

Caroline continued, "So, Josh came in, looking crazy again—you know, with that same look on his face I have described to you. Well, he started trying to hurt me, emotionally, again. And before I even had a chance to ask him to leave—he turned around and announced he was going to leave because he realized he was intolerable again. Then he smirked and packed his bag—and before you knew it—I was begging him to stay!"

Caroline felt Josh was reading her mind. I countered, "No, Josh isn't Superman. We're dealing with *a disease* that's cunning, baffling and powerful. It's alcoholism that's powerful, not Josh." I told her this, knowing she'd have to be reminded of it for months before the impact of it will begin to sink in. *Eventually, she will start to see the disease as powerful, instead of Josh.*

Then we discussed what she could have done instead of begging him to stay. She could have said simply that it was fine if he left. She didn't have to yell it, or repeat it.

When you're doing what's right for you, it's okay to say it *once,* simply, *and then refuse to discuss anything further.*

If that's a new behavior for you, and it scares you, you can leave the house or room for a while, and ask him not to be there when you get back.

If you made a mistake and asked him not to leave, you can think about what you've said and say, "No, I changed my mind. You can leave. In fact, I'd prefer it."

You don't have to debate, discuss, or retaliate to "prove" you are sane when he accuses you of not knowing what you want. The quieter you are when you put this new behavior in practice, the easier it will be on you. Afterwards—you will experience less guilt.

Most wives of alcoholics have more trouble dealing with their own guilt than with the pain from the batterings they receive. That's what keeps them stuck in old behavior patterns. You must find ways to lessen your guilt feelings.

If you don't yell, you will avoid or lessen the stomach pain and anxiety that accompanies guilt; you will be less afraid; you will *know,* in a very deep sense, that you have done what's been your best for you and your family.

And that is why it is so important for the wife to try very hard to calmly state, "No, you cannot do this to me" or "You must leave" or whatever needs to be said. This will enable her to carry through emotionally.

If you could not manage to remain calm, it is very

important that you learn *to quickly accept your humanness,* and just promise yourself to try harder to be calm, the next time. *This will help you to get rid of that destructive guilt.* You must try to remember that God is not interested in hurting you, in punishing you—your human reaction was very normal. So, take it easy on yourself. Be gentle with the person you are.

These changes are difficult, and they are going to be slow. They will be very hard at first. But it will get easier. Your guilt will ease.

Remember when the guilt sets in: You are helping your husband when you do what's right for you and him, when you say no to allowing his disease to hurt you. You are helping him not to sink deeper into his disease; therefore, you are helping him to stay alive, to get and stay sober—no matter what he says. He's too sick to understand that, too disoriented to appreciate it. Please don't expect him to understand. In fact, expect him *not* to understand. It's part of his disease. But, if you follow these ideas, you will get healthier and you will help *him* to make the choice to get well.

When my emotions are in turmoil, O God, I pray that you will be there to speak peace, healing and hope.

17

Deal With His Arrogance!

He is only a paper tiger.
The real world sees him as pathetic.
You are a lot more powerful than you think
you are.

Eight of us sat in a circle in my living room, which
also doubles as my office where I see my clients
(families of alcoholics). Rosemary flopped herself in
the rocker; Carrie sank deep in the wing chair. Both
of them bolted straight up when Madeline said she
wanted to talk about her husband's "incredible arrogance."

"He lost another job—which, by the way, I had
mixed feelings about," Madeline began explaining.
"Of course I was upset that he was getting obviously
sicker—especially when I saw that he was denying
the reason *why* he lost the job.

"He keeps saying, 'Accounting just isn't for me.'
Well, he had been an accountant for fifteen years, on
and off; and it's true that he didn't stay in one job—

he always seemed either to get fired or quit just before he *would have* gotten fired, on the pretext that 'it wasn't his kind of work.' Then he'd manage to find something else, lose that job, and it was the same thing all over again.

"And what's strange is that he'd go to an entirely different line of work, for a few years, anyway. Then he would say, 'It isn't for me,' and then he would go *back* to that first line of work he had left. He kept up this same pattern for seventeen years! He lost nine jobs in seventeen years. It would seem fine if they were his *choices*, decisions he made to try to *better* himself, but, instead, they all seemed like frantic running all the time.

"I guess what really bothers me now, though, is what I'm seeing as the reasons for all his jumping around. He lives with such hate inside him. All the time he tells me how he resents this and resents that. It really interferes with his work. He spends so much time doing what *he* wants on the job—not following orders and even deliberately disobeying them because *he* thinks he knows what's right, or because he resents the boss for having money, that he doesn't spend his time doing *his* job right. When he gets told off, it increases his resentment, and then everything goes downhill real fast."

Madeline went on, "And to tell you the whole truth, I'm upset too, because whenever I've gone to those office parties with him, he acts so weird with the women. It's kind of like a combination of being angry with them and fawning over them. He 'comes on' to them—and it's so obvious to the women, to me and everyone else—and he looks like a fool because the women are contemptuous toward him, but he doesn't seem to care. Then he gets mad because they won't play his game. He does that everywhere—at all his jobs, with our friends, everywhere.

"Then this whole thing starts to affect his work too! He comes home, and in talking with me, he 'lets it drop' that he's mad at a certain woman at work because she won't look at him and he seems to spend a lot of his days just sitting at work, and being mad—at her or somebody—anybody!

"But one of the worst times of all for me, is when, after he's lost another job—he begins a new one. For a while, at the beginning, when no one knows his game too well (he's quite charming, you know), he starts to act like he just doesn't need me around any more. He gets *so* puffed up! So arrogant!"

Everyone broke in at this point. One of the women said, "I know exactly what you mean! Every time a normally nice thing happens to my husband he acts like he's King Tut and he pretends I'm just not needed around any more!"

"My husband gets that way when a woman smiles at him. Or when a few of his drinking buddies talk about how they 'don't need their wives, any more!' Their arrogance seems to be infectious," another one wryly commented.

By the end of the session, we came up with a few guidelines that most of the people tried. They found these do work for them:

1. Remember that his period of "puffed-up time" doesn't last. It ends when his co-workers discover the "real" person underneath all the charm. It ends with the first order from authority figures being deliberately disobeyed. "I'll show 'em who's boss" behavior cannot last forever.

It ends, in essence, when they see he's a trouble-maker, when he no longer can stand the strain of looking like a "nice person," when he drops his facade.

2. As his illness progresses, it takes a shorter amount of time for him to get arrogant. It's just like the drinking; he gets sicker quicker. Whereas, before, it would take several months before he would begin his personality change on the job, now, it takes only a month or six weeks before it starts to happen.

3. Why is it such a relief to the wife when her husband can't keep up his "act" as long as he could previously? It is usually because he is so obnoxious during all this time when things are going well for him. She is afraid people think of her as less than she is because *he* looks so "terrific" and *she* is always so angry at *him. His public image is so wonderful!* She questions her own sanity—*is* he that terrific? She wishes *so much* that she could be happy for him in his new job, but his behavior cancels that possibility.

4. Remember, you've been conditioned to know that if it's going to be nice for him—as long as he

stays sick—it's going to be hell for you.

5. Just knowing that this is "typical" of many alcoholics' behavior helps you not to feel you are rotten or crazy. Most wives of alcoholics don't get so *angry* from just the drinking. It's the related behavior that gets them mad!

6. Don't reveal your fears when he acts like he doesn't need you any more. Remember you are dealing with a paper tiger.

7. If he takes you to a social gathering and acts very puffed up and pays no attention to you, don't beg him for attention. Don't sulk and look like a victim-in-the-corner. Enter into the festivities and enjoy yourself. (Two-to-one, your husband will be at your side within minutes, sulking that he wants to go home.) *Don't*. Insist on staying awhile. Leave later—slowly, reluctantly, with a lot of smiles.

These tactics are harmless in themselves, *because you know your motives*. You are not being cruel—you're helping him. You cannot afford to be victimized any longer. It's not good for you, nor for him, if he succeeds in making a victim out of you. *He has to see that the people he tries to smash won't stand for it, any more*.

Not every alcoholic is arrogant. But if yours is, his behavior in this area can be among the most emotionally painful ones you have to contend with.

Try to remember that everyone who lives with an alcoholic has areas that need to be dealt with. Some can't stand it when their husbands don't bring in enough to feed all the kids; others face the problem of other women; others must cope with gambling. In addition, many wives face arrogance and incredibly debilitating put-downs from their alcoholic husbands.

Realizing that these things are only symptoms of his disease helps. However, you don't have to learn how to "figure around it." Neither do you need to learn how to "cope" with *his* problem. Learn, instead, how to go *beyond* his problems, not taking the consequences of his behavior. Life is too short to be living in a practice hell. You have a right to get *his* monkey off *your* back.

I pray for the realization that I can live no one's life but my own.

18
Don't Change Your Address!

Booze is everywhere.
Running increases panic.
Running helps him to continue to deny.

One woman reports that her husband wants her to leave their "pesky" five-year-old with her folks and move to Alaska. This is his answer to losing his seventh job in five years.

Another wife tells me her husband says the answer lies in moving back to the hills of West Virginia where he was born. *But* she should move there and wait for him. He's in the navy for another three years, stationed in Hawaii. (I guess he's supposed to get sober through some kind of osmosis. If *she's* in them thar hills, he will get the message.)

Still another wife of an alcoholic reports her hubby came home, after being absent without a word for five days, and proudly announced the purchase of their new house trailer, waiting on the shores of Virginia Beach. The only requirement? She must dump her job and their kids and move there with him.

Sometimes if the alcoholic is feeling generous, he doesn't mind taking the kids along. All you have to do, then, is leave your job, friends, family, roots—in a frantic scramble for the "right" place for him to find sobriety.

Wives often cry, "I tried so hard to eliminate all the things that make him drink!"

I know it makes you feel you're close to your husband when you both plan and work together to try to find out how to lick this drinking problem. But it's a false closeness. It's really a collusion to avoid the real help.

The outside world doesn't make him drink.

Problems don't make him drink. If they did, everybody would be an alcoholic.

In-laws don't make him drink. If they did, all married people would be alcoholics.

His being so "sensitive" doesn't make him drink. Yes, he's sensitive. He's sensitive to booze! He has an allergy and an addiction to alcohol, and that's what makes him drink—his disease.

You can't kill off the world.
You can't destroy every bar.
You can't erase all his problems.
The world is never "just right."

You can't be sure that if you move to the country, they won't someday rezone the region and build a bar right next-door.

The sooner you get off this merry-go-round of trying to help him find yet another way other than A.A. for his problem, the sooner he will have a chance to get sober. Can you imagine a family with a father who has diabetes running around trying to find a place in which to live where there's no sugar, disrupting their entire lives, instead of just insisting that he must take his insulin?

Your husband's insulin is Alcoholics Anonymous.

Stop helping him to continue to deny. Moving to the country won't help.

Let me see life more clearly by capturing the present moment.

19

Hide the Car Keys?

Let go, and let God.
You must do what is least uncomfortable for you.

The title poses a ticklish question.

Experts run the gamut on this question. Some advise, "Keep your hands totally off his problem, and that includes the car keys. Just don't get in that car, yourself, or don't let the kids ride with him, when he's been drinking." Others suggest, "Keep your hands off his problem, except when it involves saving *other* people's lives on the road."

Whichever advice you decide to follow, please keep in mind several crucial factors:

1. If *you* are going to get well—get over the terrible mental effects of this disease on yourself—you *must* learn to get out of his business *entirely*. If you feel you should take the car keys, do it after you have reached enough emotional distance from his problem, that your action won't drag you "back in there." And make sure your motivation isn't that

you can "get back in there" and become involved with him again.

2. If you're going to hide the keys, do it with as little fanfare as possible. Just hide them, *and then forget it. If you think you can't carry this off effectively to save your own emotional and physical well-being, don't do it.*

3. If you're scared he might hit you, or if you're going to be frightened of him at all, don't take the keys.

4. Most people, if they haven't lived with alcoholism, don't understand the complications that develop when the wife "does something so simple as taking the car keys when he's been drinking." They don't understand that the implications of this act are far-reaching. They don't understand that this can easily get her much more embroiled in his problem, get her deeper into the sickness. They don't see that her main job is to get detached—for when *she* becomes detached and healthy, her *kids* will—and, hopefully, so will her husband. So every "little" action has to be looked at by this one question: Will this get the wife *more* involved with his disease or *less*?

If taking those car keys gets her more involved with him, then, I'd say, "Let go and let God."

God, help me to trust my capability to cope and to conquer because your power enables me to be strong.

20

You Have the Right
To Get Sick Too!

He expects that he will always "make mistakes."
He expects that you will never fail him.

"Sobriety means getting rid of the bottle *and* the baby." Those words are from a physician who directs a fine alcoholism treatment center. What does he mean? The still-sick alcoholic not only has a problem with alcohol, but with immaturity—to the point of *infantile* social behavior.

One of the ways this irresponsibility manifests itself is in the alcoholic's high degree of selfishness—an infantile narcissism which means that, after the booze, *he* is the important one. It's a long way down the line before anyone or anything else is truly important, except that which helps him get momentarily puffed up—serving his illusions of grandeur. This is not an exaggeration of facts, merely a statement of them as they are, part and parcel of his disease.

So what does this have to do with why he runs off when *you* get sick? After all you've done for him—through all the crazy behaviors of *his* illness—he gets upset when you even get the *flu!* You worry, and with good reason: If you should *really* get sick some day in your life—who would take care of you?

Unfortunately, the facts don't seem to indicate he's going to, on his own, have a great change of heart and become a caring person. The facts say he is a very sick man, not just occasionally, but always, as long as he drinks—and that his disease is a *progressive* one. This means he will most definitely be getting sicker if he does not get well. It further means he will be in even worse shape to help you, should you become ill.

There is one paradoxical fact that could, and would improve the situation *for you*. The sooner you stop centering your life around him; the sooner you give his whole disease back to him; the sooner you let go of his problem; the better chances will be that he will treat *you* well!

How do you get to that place where you stop being the caretaker? Start practicing the ideas in this book. Go to Al-Anon, a therapist, someone who's going to help you to become the person you deserve to be! You *don't* want to wind up embittered and possibly helpless.

I am determined, O God, to make this day a happy one.

21
Learn About Blackouts

It's like being unconscious—while fully awake.
It's like amnesia, afterwards.

Jan's husband, Bob, relates this story: "I started to know I was in trouble with my drinking when I had started off, one weekend, to go to the shore, and wound up at an airport on Monday morning. I thought I was at Kennedy Airport—but I was at the San Francisco Airport!

"And I wasn't passed out when I went through that weekend. I was *moving!* But I don't remember a thing."

Blackouts

Most homicides occur between people who know each other—while under the influence of a drug, such as alcohol. (Eighty percent of the people in jail committed crimes while drugged.) Many of these convicted felons truly do not remember committing crimes.

During a blackout, a person *seems,* to everyone,

93

including himself, to be fully aware of what he is doing—many even appear to be fully in control.

How can you know when your husband is having a blackout? There is no way. The only way for anyone to know is if, at a later time, you are both talking about something he said or did before, and he seems surprised, denies it and looks truly scared that either you or he is crazy—it probably signals that a blackout has occurred.

What do you do then? First, you must tell him what really happened. Call or bring other people in to confirm the truth—people he will believe, if possible.

This *might* be the time to confront him about his problem.

(Meanwhile, call Alcoholics Anonymous and ask them to send you a meeting schedule for your area, and some literature. Write to Narcotics Education, Inc. [Box 4390/ Tacoma Park, Maryland 20912] and ask for a specific booklet, "Brain Damage Starts With the First Drink." If your husband is receptive, you'll have it to offer to him to read.)

Then drop it. Don't harangue or repeat yourself. Simply leave the room—or the house, if the temptation to preach at him gets too great. This could be a crucial moment, if he has been receptive, and if you've quietly said what you had to say.

If he seems open and receptive to the idea of getting help—if he says so—give him the A.A. phone number in your area. (It will be on the literature you receive.) The telephone operator has A.A. numbers also. *But let him make the call.*

And if he balks? If he refuses? Hold your temper. You've made your point. His drinking will get scarier from now on. You've helped crack through much of his denial. Now, just get out of the room, and at least *act as if* it really doesn't affect you at all. *If he sees you worrying, he will figure he doesn't need to.*

During a blackout, he may promise something to the children, and then forget his promise—maybe a camping trip. When the time comes, the children will get ready and say, "Come on, dad!" He actually will not know what they're talking about. He may get mad at you and at them, thinking everybody's trying to drive him crazy, "with all their accusations."

What do you do in a case like this? Again, you must confront him by telling him that he did, indeed, make the promise. And let *him* face the consequences of that with the kids. Let *them* confront him with broken promises.

Later, tell the children about his disease, if they don't know about it already. Explain to them about blackouts. Tell them they have a right to be angry at being disappointed, but then show them how futile it is to stay mad at a *disease*. Offer to take them to Al-Ateen, (or pre-Teen) if they're between six and nineteen years old. (The telephone operator has the phone number of Al-Ateen; or call Al-Anon, and get it.)

Now, what else can you do? Get busy and be good to yourself the rest of this day—and every day—one day at a time.

The role of victim is not a very pleasant one. Please show me the way to learn a new role in life.

22

Try To Remember It's a Disease

But it doesn't mean you have to accept unaccept-
able behavior.
Don't punish the alcoholic; it will only add to your
guilt.
Don't pity the alcoholic; it will only lead you back
into rescuing him.

When Joanne came into treatment for herself and
her kids because *they* were going crazy from Tom
(her husband) who was the alcoholic, she got furious
when she heard that he had a disease—instead of just
being a no-good, drunken bum.

"Oh, now he's got an excuse! He's sick! Now he
can get drunk and we're supposed to say, 'Oh, that
poor sick guy. He has an addiction. He can't help it.
It's bigger than he is.' We're not even allowed to get
mad any more. You feel so crummy being angry at a
sick person. But I'm still mad. I just submerge it and
get depressed."

I told her to hold it right there. Yes, he's sick. And
he can't stop too easily after he takes that first drink.

But he does have a choice of whether or not to pick up that first drink. And he does have the choice of whether or not to get help that would give him the support he needs to stay sober.

Joanne broke in, "Okay I see that. But, meanwhile, while he's still out there drinking, and he comes home and he starts his 'stuff', and he won't stop, I do react even though I try not to. I count to ten to get detached—but he follows me around and tries to get my goat. And then I blow! I let out all the stuff I've been storing up—and then I feel so guilty when I realize I've been whipping him and he looks so pitiful, like a beaten dog. He cries and tells me how bad he is and how he doesn't know how I put up with him and how he deserves every bit of what I say, and more—and then I feel worse. And then I get *so* mad and feel so despairing. What can I *do?*"

"Try to avoid the two p's," I suggested. "Punish and pity. He certainly doesn't need punishment. It just adds to his despair and feelings of unworthiness and self-denigration. But the main reason not to punish him is for *yourself*—God certainly is not going to punish you for yelling at him when any 'normal' person would get mad enough to hit him under those same circumstances! But yelling is not effective. It will not make him truly repentant. It will not get him sober. And it just increases your guilt."

And in a strange way, he likes to be yelled at! If you reinforce his behavior (reward it) with attention—then, he gets the attention he's seeking. It's like a child having a tantrum. You don't get mad at the child; you simply ignore his behavior. The child soon learns that a tantrum is not an effective way to get attention or any other thing he wants. Do the same with the "junk" the alcoholic chooses to say. Tell yourself, "My alcoholic is getting into his junk-talk behavior. I will not reward it with my attention." Go about your business. Buy earplugs, if necessary. Tune him out as best you can. Leave the house for an hour or so, if you must or want to—but leave with a smile, so he believes he is not "getting to you." Do this often enough and his junk behavior will fade, because it gets no reward. In this way, you will be giving his disease the attention it deserves: *none*.

What about pity? Teachers of "disturbed children" for a long time have known about the concept of self-fulfilling prophecy. If you act like a child is too pitiful to succeed, he probably won't. If you just don't pay attention to his former track record—and if you act as if that child is average and will perform as well as any other and you treat him that way—he will have a good chance at success. The same applies to the alcoholic. Alcoholics often have an uncanny ability to "come through" and deal well with situations in which a family member feels *in the inner gut,* that the alcoholic *will* be able to cope.

The family gets in trouble when they don't entirely believe they have the *right* to expect a certain behavior. For instance, if the spouse *believes* she could not even *conceive* of her husband not paying the telephone bill—he most likely will pay it. If, on the other hand, a wife is nervous and gets really angry and bemoans her husband's not paying the bills and confront him angrily and *fearfully,* then it comes through that she really does not believe he will do it—and he probably won't. It comes back to the bottom line which is upgrading the alcoholic's self-esteem.

In other words, keep your compassion, but keep it at a "clinical distance." Understand that your job is to be an effective, comfortable, deserving wife or husband. And your spouse, alcoholic or not, must come through with the same things you would expect from any "normal" husband or wife. To expect less is to treat him like an emotional cripple; and that is degrading to both of you. Rescuing someone keeps them dependent on you; it preserves a neurotic relationship. It may make you feel comfortable for a time, but that person will grow to resent you later.

Alcoholics, like any other people, know the difference between you making excuses for them ("Oh, he's so sick"), and doing for them what they should do for themselves—always sacrificing, sacrificing, sacrificing. The more you act with this lack of self-respect, the less respect the alcoholic will have for you. *How many doormats do you admire?* When was the last time you saw a person who acted like a doormat and you said to yourself, "Now, there's an admirable person."

Courage is fear that has said its prayers.

23
Let the Crises Happen

They might save his life.
They will save your sanity.

Crises often occur in the alcoholic's life when: he can't get up in the morning because the hangover's too horrible, and he's already on probation at work; your husband asks you to call in sick for him; it's chilly outside and he has passed out on the porch; he's in jail and wants you to bail him out; he promised something to the kids and forgot; he's out of booze and wants you to go to the store

There's a lot more you could add to the list. A crisis occurs for the alcoholic when his disease is in trouble—when his disease cries out for you to intervene and help. These crises happen so often that you probably live in a constant state of excited misery.

There was a time, several years ago, when authorities in the field of alcoholism believed that a family member had to "create the crisis." As professionals realized how frequently these crises occurred, beliefs changed to: Just let them happen!

What *does* happen when the wife lets a hurtful thing happen to the alcoholic, without stepping in and rescuing him, like she used to?

She feels guilty.

The alcoholic gets angry and threatens her.

That's when the real crisis begins—for her.

If she can go through with her plan to do what she knows is necessary for her, him, and the children, despite his threats, and despite her feelings of fear, anger and depression—and act self-protectively in the process—then the wife is well on the road to her own recovery from his insane behavior.

Karen is a client of mine who is *so* calm, now! She's a veteran of these "wars" with his disease.

Karen told the therapy group: "The main thing I think is important is that after you go through this the first time, and you think you'll never be able to do it—you'll never be able to get through the fears and the threats—you find that you *do* get through it, that you *get* stronger, that it *wasn't* as bad as you thought it would be for you. The next time it's easier. And then, from then on, it gets so much easier, you can't believe it! Before you know it, you're detached from his problems, and you're living calmly, serenely, *and you're not scared of him any more.* All I know is that it does happen that way. It happened for me and you never met a bigger coward, a more scared woman who was afraid of losing her alcoholic husband to another woman, than I was. *I* lost *my* fears! I *know* you can!"

Karen's case is not unusual. There are over 100,000 Al-Anon groups around the world—plus other therapy groups for wives of alcoholics—with over a million women participating. All these wives have problems in common with yours. Almost without fail, if they keep trying, if they use the knowledge they've learned, they do not fail in getting healed from the wounds inflicted on them by their husband's alcoholism. They get stronger; they're no longer at the mercy of their husbands' disease.

DO'S AND DON'TS:

Let his crises happen to him. Let him—not you—take the consequences of his disease.

Don't pick up the pieces of his falling-apart life.

If he loses a job or his driver's license—rejoice! It means he's getting sicker, quicker. It means that maybe he won't be able to stand up to that disease much longer.

Don't get scared if he seems to recuperate quickly from his crises and "looks good" afterwards, like nothing's happened. He may even smile and whistle and act like he's getting better instead of sicker! Don't be fooled by that! It's all part and parcel of his denial system. Inside, he's scared to death, because his disease is progressing, if he isn't recovering. Stop believing his bluffs—they are just "his disease talking."

What do you do when other people rescue him after you've stopped?

This commonly happens! Doctors, ministers, counselors—unwitting enablers—very often feel sorry and believe the lies his disease creates. His mother, sister, brother, his boss, his "friends" who drink with him—many people get sucked in and cooperate with him, not realizing they are being manipulated and are helping to keep him sick. The alcoholic usually has a whole string of patsies who believe his half-truths, his innocent understatements of what he really does, his denial system.

What can you do?

1. *If* any one of them is willing to calmly discuss the problem with you privately, give them this book to read, ask them to attend Al-Anon and/or other therapy with you, to truly learn how to help the alcoholic.

2. Try to remember that if those others *must*—for their own guilt or need to control—rescue your husband, they will probably get tired of his "junk" just like you did. They will probably see through him eventually, especially if you keep your hands off! *Nothing seems to "fire-up" a new rescuer more than an irate wife who insists that the person is a fool!* Don't give such people a chance to get mad at you and to try even harder, therefore, to show that

they're right—not you!

3. His disease is getting worse and more people will see through him quicker—despite seemingly occasional bursts of his "looking so good."

4. Don't expect his other rescuers to like you or approve of you when *you* stop rescuing him.

Remember these things. They'll help calm you when you're furious and scared. Do what *you* have to do.

You do not have to discuss, explain, or defend your behavior to others, no matter what their "credentials" are! Just do your part, and you'll feel good about yourself.

And if he chooses to get well, he will drop all his sick friends and be your *husband*, not a cripple who needs twenty mommies.

If a crisis happens, help my perspective to remain clear and my emotions to be strong.

24

No More Lying To His Boss!

Losing his job may be just what he needs to want sobriety.
Every time you let go of his problem, you get healthier.

Alcoholics Anonymous tells its members to "think the drink through." *The "drinks" of the spouse of the alcoholic—the actions she compulsively takes that keep her addicted to her husband—are those that keep her involved in his alcoholism, that keep her sick right along with him.*

Those "drinks" are often rescuing tactics which may include covering up for him. So, instead of merely suggesting that you don't tell the boss that he's "sick," I'd like to discuss the consequences of your rescuing him.

Sure, it's easier in the short run to tell the boss it's the "flu." Why? Your guilt is alleviated temporarily. Your anxieties about the gas bill and electric bill, the phone cutoff notice—are alleviated temporarily. You kid yourself into thinking that since you stuck by him again, this might make his love so strong, he will stop drinking. Also, he will *see* this time, what a good woman you are.

What's really going on? It's perfectly natural to be anxious and angry about those bills. It's absolute baloney that he will wake up after this episode and be any better off. *He's getting sicker if he's not sober.* Your actions are just prolonging the agony for him— just putting off the day when he *has* to get well or die. But the longer he stays in his illness, the less chance for recovery he has. The more entrenched the illness becomes, the more a toll on his body and brain it will take. So, helping him to stay drunk (and that's what a rescue operation is) is helping him to get deeper into his illness. But what's it doing to you? It's helping you to get deeper into his illness and making you sicker from it.

Each time you act like it's okay to save him from the consequences of his behavior, you are pretending you are powerful enough to save him from his disease. You may *say* you understand it's a disease and that you are powerless over it, *but your actions belie this. What you do is what you believe.*

If you now say, "You're right. This is no good for him. I can see that now. But what about me? I need those bills paid, even if it means he gets sicker. I don't want to lose the mortgage!"

You're right. But start to take action based on

reality from now on:

1. Start to *believe* the facts about this disease: your saving his job is a stopgap measure. If he's losing time from his job, face the facts—he might be fired due to his drinking. All the excuses in the world aren't going to help the boss accept all those times off.

2. Facing these facts also means *taking action* to save yourself and your children. One client of mine insisted to her husband that the house be put in her name only. He knew that what he was doing might result in them becoming homeless, so he agreed. Your husband may not agree; but it's an idea to suggest. Even if he rejects it today, he may agree later.

3. Another very positive action you can take is to get yourself a job skill, if you don't have a paying job already. Go to a Manpower Center, a Women's Training Center, take a free course. Learn a job skill you can use in an office or at home. If your kids are small, you can put signs up, advertising your services of typing or catering. You don't have to pay for advertising. Call the nearby college. Put a notice in their newspaper. Put signs up at laundromats. Put notices on bulletin boards.

4. But what can you do for money *now*? Be resourceful. Can you take care of children? Take in three children and provide cookies, milk, games, light lunches. Make sure you take them early enough for the parent to go to work. And keep the children till 6:00 P.M. when the parents get off work. Any day

care that provides an eight-and-a-half-hour day for the child is welcome. Not all do.

5. Stash some money away, every week, in a savings account in your name only. It is insanity for the wife of an alcoholic not to have emergency food money for her and the children. It is not rotten or mean. It is sane. Feeding the children comes before money for a disease.

SUMMARY: Alcoholism has to be faced. You can only escape the consequences of his disease when you start to coolly evaluate the situation. You may still have tremendous resentment that stops you from doing anything to save yourself—that can stop you from doing anything but saying, "He'd better just stop all this!" Continuing to believe his promises, crying, threatening, going into a constant cycle of depression, explosion, anxiety, guilt—is that what you want out of life? It will only get worse if you don't get off this merry-go-round. It won't change him—because you're railing against a disease.

And *is* he getting away with not facing his responsibilities? Look at him. Is that sodden man—unconscious half the time—is that *dying* man getting away with anything?

God, help me to cling to you instead of my problems.

25

Start To Get Help—
Even Though He's the Drunk

If you live with insanity long enough, you: a. feel insane, b. act insane.

Each time I talked with Marla, she would say she would think about getting help for herself. It was on her mind; it bothered her; it angered her that she should need help. I was concerned for her, but she didn't feel she needed therapy.

But she was hurting.

Marla and I met at a workshop I gave for a treatment center. She came up to me afterwards, and we talked. I watched her, listened to her, and asked her, "Are you the daughter of an alcoholic?"

She answered, "Yes," and she was obviously startled.

Marla is very dramatic; she exaggerates everything, both good and bad. She thinks life is boring if it isn't full of "marvelous ups and downs." She has a mercurial personality: all or nothing. She's a perfectionist; when she does something well, she feels like she's on top of the world, can lick anything; and when things aren't going fast enough for her super-fast pace, she's in the pits.

Marla is what is known as a co-alcoholic:

People who live with alcoholism long enough develop personality traits much like the alcoholic's—except for the addiction to alcohol.

Children of alcoholics often wind up with a "co-alcoholic personality"—and keep those behavior patterns *long* after they've left home.

Those children—more than half of them—marry alcoholics and/or become alcoholics themselves.

What if you're the spouse or the child of an alcoholic and you have developed behavior patterns that are disturbing *to you*?

I know you have these "personality problems" because you live with "him."

I know you have a nervous stomach or migraines or sleeplessness because you live in a crazy household.

But you're still hurting.

Your parents could die or be dead already; your husband could die from alcoholism or go crazy from a "wet brain." But *you* will still hurt from your learned behavior patterns unless you get help.

Sallyann came to four sessions of the therapy group and was doing fine but then she stopped.

Herman, her husband, was gloating about "her

sickness." It got her so mad. After all, *he* was the one who kept having "slips" and getting drunk and then getting back into A.A. and getting drunk again.

Her husband "got to her" in two ways: he put her down for being so sick, for "needing more help than him." And he upped his "games" with other women every time she attended a therapy session, in order to scare her into not going.

What's Sallyann's problem?

She's letting him determine whether she's going to get the help she needs in order to stop feeling bad. She's letting him emotionally blackmail her into thinking that "she's weak" for getting help. She's still revolving around the alcoholic.

Marla covers up her problem by bluffing—intellectualizing. She is mortified that "I saw through her and easily saw character traits, as if she were so transparent," she tells me. What Marla doesn't see is that she is so *very* everything—so un-bland in her personality—that *everybody* obviously sees her traits! She encourages them to see, *really* see her, in fact. A therapist who works regularly with families of alcoholics can easily recognize behavior patterns in those families and can readily "spot" someone who grows up and/or lives with alcoholism.

What was bothering Marla then? It came down to this: she didn't mind coming off as being flamboyant, intriguing, etc. What annoyed her was that others saw it as a combination of problems arising from her association with alcoholism. Not just her "unique," marvelous, dramatic personality.

I further explained this to Marla—and this helped to quell her fears that my observations were in any way saying she wasn't "interesting." I told her that I was concerned that these very things she cultivated in herself were the same characteristics that kept her feeling bad: the ups and downs that were constant; the need to "be in the spotlight"; the dread of being an average person.

When Marla finally did come to therapy, she started seeing that a lot of her behaviors were over-compensation—that she was, as she laughingly called it, "an egomaniac with an inferiority complex!" When Marla got to the place where she felt good about herself, when she stopped needing to *prove* she was terrific to everyone, Marla started liking the idea of "averageness," of "normalcy." It meant *peace*. It did *not* mean she had to stop being creative. It did mean she didn't have to have painful side effects.

She learned to "take the edges off" her ups and downs. She learned to "catch herself" when she found herself getting too *anything*: too happy; too sad; too involved or too attached. She learned to "let go" of a lot of her dependence on outside people and events. She learned how to find inner peace.

But she first had to get help.

She had to overcome her pride that said, "I'm not in trouble; I'm interesting and my life is complicated; that's all."

And Sallyann? She had to get to the point where she went to therapy *not for her alcoholic, but for herself*.

In listening to Sallyann in the group, we found that she had been married to two troubled men in the past, both of whom she "suspected" were alcoholics. Sallyann had "had it up to here" trying to find out ways to help her husbands. But the problem was that Sallyann was always in therapy in order to learn how to adjust to their craziness, to learn how to "make him behave." Naturally, her therapists tried to help Sallyann see the folly of this. But she always quit therapy, depressed and frustrated that she didn't succeed in making her husband better. Sallyann had to hurt enough, just like the alcoholic does, in order to get help for *herself*—to get over the wounds she received from her various husbands' alcoholisms.

What if *you're* still balking at getting help to improve your life?

Remember:

1. It's not going to get better. It's going to get worse. His disease is progressive.

2. You're not committed to a life sentence of living in insanity.

3. You don't have to get to the point of suicide or a nervous breakdown to get help. *That won't punish him!* On the contrary, he will just get mad at you for it. That's part of his disease's usual reaction to the wife or kids getting sick.

4. Don't go down the tubes for, or with your alcoholic. If he decides to get well, where will you be?

Thank you for showing me I need not suffer from another's illness.

26

Stay With Him or Leave Him "Just for Today"

Don't be angry with yourself for not having left him before.

You have more options than you think:

    You can stay, and leave the room or the house, for a while.

    You can leave for a few days.

    You can leave for weeks or months and see your spouse when you want to.

    You'll think of many more choices when you remember that your alcoholic needs you very much, even though he denies it.

Marsha used to leave Phil all the time, in order to punish him. She'd wind up scared, depressed, and go back in worse shape than when she left. It never worked the way it was supposed to. It didn't make him "act right," and since Marsha didn't carry through with her threats, Phil became more arrogant and Marsha felt furious, terrified and trapped.

Sharon never left. But she always threatened to leave. Her alcoholic husband "upped the ante" and left her for a while. He came back, but it scared her so much that she never threatened or did anything again that crossed him. Needless to say, he got worse and left more often, enjoying her fear of him and his sense of power. Sharon didn't know about alcoholism; she didn't realize her husband only *acted* so independent because he was so terrified of his really dependent nature. *He* knew he was more dependent on Sharon than she was on him. *Keeping her scared was his way of trying to smash her down enough so she wouldn't find out she didn't need him as much as she thought she did.*

The maddening fact in the alcoholic family is that the spouse seems so vulnerable to the alcoholic's threats, and the alcoholic seems so invulnerable to hers. Most of the threats seem to get down to this basic one: abandonment combined with humiliation. What can the spouse do? Here are some sanity-saving suggestions:

1. *Make yourself emotionally comfortable.* This takes courage, for if you make yourself comfortable, your alcoholic will start to make those "little" threats again. But he will do it anyway. You can't please him. It's a no-win situation. If you try to please him, you'll get hurt by him anyway and have a resentment which only hurts you: "After all I tried to help him, he turned around and hurt me anyway when he *promised* he wouldn't!" Even if your alcoholic wants

117

to be nice to you for a time, his sickness makes him stubborn too. He *won't* please you and he will tell you again that "no one's going to tell me what to do!" (Telling him what to do usually entails asking him to be nice to you, not to hurt you.) But every time you beg, threaten, or connive to get your alcoholic to make you happy, you are giving him the power to make you unhappy. The truth is he won't use that power to make you happy—he'll use that power to make you unhappy. Take that power back. You're *not* the frightened child who is at his mercy that you think you are; and he is not the movie star, the tin god, you think he is. All those thoughts are part of the insanity in an alcoholic home.

How does he lose his power to hurt you? Sometimes, if all other suggestions in this book don't work for the immediate crisis and fear, remember you have a right to walk away from threats, embarrassment, and the ever-present insecurities *that your alcoholic husband makes you think you should learn to live with*. A normal husband doesn't act that way: he tries to make his wife feel cherished and secure. (You need to hear this, for by now you probably think it's the other way around: that *you've* got to make everything all right all the time so he won't hurt you again.)

2. *Act as if you are not scared of his retaliations.* ("I'll never let you back in the house again"; "I'll see other women"; "You'll be sorry—I'll get well and make another woman happy.") Act unafraid long

118

enough, and you will become unafraid.

3. *Remember it's just his disease talking.* If you have left him for a while and are wanting to see him (you feel you can handle it), and if he gets arrogant and tells you he's not sure he needs you any more, remember it's just his disease talking. Pretend he's a casual friend who's busy when you called her to go shopping and answer him the way you would answer her: "Okay. See you!" Wave off; be breezy and nice and don't act devastated. Eventually, you will actually feel that way! And your husband will have a new respect for you.

Sophie left her husband eight months ago. She sees him now, when she wants to, and not always when he first asks to see her. If she anticipates more pain than she thinks she can handle or wants to deal with, she just tells him she can't make it that particular time. She sees her husband as a date for that day or weekend. If he is good to her, fine; if he is nasty to the point of exasperation for her, she merely leaves. Then she goes on with her life, thinking of her needs and doing what is good for her, blocking out thoughts of her alcoholic. She enjoys the peace in her alone life now. Sophie has lost her fears. When her Harold makes the ultimate threat of finding "someone else," (even in subtle ways, he has threatened this), she told me that she tells herself, "If my Harold had any other disease—T.B., for instance— he would not threaten me that when he gets well and gets out of the sanitarium, he will leave me. That's all part and parcel of the insanity of his alcoholism."

When Martha temporarily left her alcoholic, she started to be with him some weekends. Sometimes her husband would get to be "too much" for her; he would play his usual games and she would react. When she fearfully called him during the week, he announced that he didn't know if he "could take" her yelling when he hurt her; "he would only see her if she shaped up." Well, Martha *was* getting well, despite temporary setbacks; she thought about his crazy threats, and she decided not to beg for a weekend with him. She began to realize she wasn't losing anything; if her husband was still sick enough to play these games, the old fears she used to have of losing him to other women seemed silly. What would they be getting? (*Her* insanity, she began to see, was in *believing* he could be crazy with her one minute and a wonderful and good husband to another woman, the next minute.) She kept telling herself, "Sane men don't emotionally threaten their wives all the time; and if he's acting insanely, why do I see him as a god, instead of a man who's ill and not powerful at all?"

4. *Do what is good for you.* You can stay; you can leave; you can go back; you can leave again; you can do anything that truly makes you comfortable. You have that right. If you can get calm in your home, fine; if you can't, fine. Very few people *could* stay sane in your home. You are not a failure.

5. *Use your today.* The next time you feel trapped in your situation, ask yourself, "Do I want to stay

with my husband, *just for today*?" Then, whether you stay or leave, *use your today*. Do one thing, today, that will get you closer to peace. Go back in the book and choose one thing you couldn't do before, one thing you think you might be able to do, at least partially. If you try to do this today and every day, whether you stay with the alcoholic or not, you will become less and less afraid, and then you will not be afraid of what he will do, any more.

Help me to no longer be manipulated by the needs of another. Let my compassion guide me to make good decisions.

27

Break Out of Your Isolation

*It will help you get an emotional distance.
You'll start to be able to make rational decisions
again.*

The craziness starts in different ways. Often, it appears in a loving guise: your alcoholic husband suggests that you go live in the country, just the two of you, in a cabin with a fireplace and no telephone. Very romantic. You cry, out of joy. "He really does need me!" "He says it will help him stay sober!" *That's the clincher.*

Maria and Cliff did just that: they scrimped and saved for twelve years—him working, her working, six kids, him drinking so that any extra money went down the drain—and all *her* paycheck went toward that cabin. She hated her job at that time; she resented that they made so much that "normal" couples would be able to get decent furniture and go to the movies regularly, but not them. It went down the toilet for booze. But that cabin got paid off.

So how did it turn out? It's a lovely place; it's worth five times what they paid for it now. But Cliff goes there every weekend—to drink.

And he "upped" the demand—it got crazier. Now he wants her to dump the kids and just come to live with him in the cabin. She thinks he's insane. "*Dump* the children?!" Those are the words he used when he snarled resentfully talking about their teen-agers. He *claims* he's only saying it because "they're so ungrateful anyway." Cliff often tells his wife he doesn't need her (when things go well for him for a few days or weeks); it's just as often that he can't even share her with their children, because he feels so threatened that he will lose her.

Howard is like that with Sarina, except that they don't have kids around any more. Their children are grown. Sarina would love to get a dog, maybe two. She would like to see a lovable animal cheer up their tension-filled home. For years Howard had said he wouldn't have a pet because it cost too much, and what would they do when vacation time came—or even when they wanted to get away for a weekend? He later told her he was too upset at the idea of sharing her even with an animal.

Marvin tried a different tack with Corinne. They had seven children and she wasn't about to dump them for anybody! Nor was she going to give up their wonderful, big Old English sheepdog. Or the five cats. Corinne was a pretty feisty lady. It took a lot to get to her "jugular," her vulnerability. But Marvin got there—and most alcoholics are able to find the vulnerabilities of their spouses in an effort to manipulate them.

His method was so bizarre that Corinne could see through it—but it didn't stop her from hurting and reacting and falling into his trap. What did he do? He called her best girlfriend—whom he never had met—under the guise of finding out what to get Corinne for her birthday—and talked real chummy. This caught Corinne's girlfriend off her guard. Marvin then called Corinne into the room to join in the "funny" conversation, and he proceeded to bring the subject around to sex in general, then to *his* sexual experiences in particular. From that point, the conversation turned to the girlfriend's problems while Marvin listened under the guise of help and sympathy. Marvin then got off the phone and told Corinne he was so turned on to the girlfriend that he had "this irrational, irresistible, yes, shamedfaced urge to go to bed with her."

Corinne, dignified, "liberated," tough lady she was, "understood" him. She tried to "discuss" with him the "why" of this attraction.

What's the point? Marvin's method worked. It was four months before Corinne called her girlfriend again.

Alcoholism is called the lonely disease.

But most people think only the alcoholic is lonely. If they think the wife might be lonely, they usually only think of her loneliness as occurring because of her "not wanting the neighbors to find out," so she keeps the curtains drawn, keeps her head down and doesn't talk, just mumbles hello at women down the street. They usually think she's just lonely because he's out drinking, or on one of his "vacations" that he just "spontaneously" takes, refusing to include her or the kids. They think she's just lonely when he doesn't show up at the maternity ward, at the children's weddings, at family reunions.

They don't realize that even though she *is* lonely at these times, *she is also lonely because she has isolated herself. She has cut herself off from others because he told her he would get sober if she got rid of everyone and everything else in her life but him.*

The horrible irony of it all is that the more she did these things to try to please him, the more contemptuous he became toward her for being such a so-easily-pushed-around person. And when he couldn't stand his own guilt any more for what he knew he was doing to her, even though he outwardly denied it, he dumped her. And by then, *he had to deny his contempt for himself,* so he believed he had all this contempt for her, for putting up with all his "stuff." But the problem for Maria, Sarina and Corinne was that they didn't understand all this. They only believed *they* were the failures. They saw the alcoholic's contempt, but they didn't see that it stemmed from his contempt for himself first. They swallowed the big lie: the big illusion that alcoholics and wives of alcoholics often live under—that if she tries real hard and can't please him, and if he leaves her, subsequently, she is a terrific failure—a wreck of a woman—*a rejected wife of an alcoholic.*

She takes all the blame: *she* was supposed to hold this marriage together, she thinks. *She forgets he's crazy. She forgets his cruelty. She forgets she's attractive, nice, intelligent.* She only believes what this alcoholic is telling her in so many words: you are worthless as a woman. *She lets a crazy man determine the way she values herself.* Things are that much out of proportion.

If it's reached this stage, or if you're getting hints that "your marriage will be saved if you just do—" (one of these self-isolating things), *stop now.* It's never too late for the wife to regain her sanity; to start to learn how to feel worthwhile. But first get off that treadmill of isolation. And don't be scared that he will leave you, even though he threatens it. Remember: if you do what the alcoholic says, all those crazy things, because you're scared of abandonment and/or humiliation, you might wind up without him at all—but if you follow a sane course and do what regular, normal people do: keep the kids, get dogs, see your friends—then, paradoxically, your chances of losing him greatly diminish! In fact, he will threaten, but his threats will be only paper-tiger threats. He will admire you for it; your value will shoot up in his eyes. He will see, in other words, that you're not afraid of losing him. And therefore you won't lose him.

Most important, you won't lose your self-respect. And if you just act *one time* out of self-respect instead of fear, you will feel more terrific inside than you've probably felt in years. And this assurance will build. You will want to act that way again. You will eventually get to the point where feeling good about yourself will be *much* more important than keeping insanity going.

Show me how to regain my self-assurance and to be happy with the uniqueness of me.

28
Stop Asking Permission!

It feels good temporarily—it makes you feel secure and "taken care of"—but it's still an illusion.

It's your way of trying to please him and keep him pleased so he won't be nasty or drink any more— but it doesn't work.

It's not as scary as you think to start to learn to stand on your feet—not his—for emotional security.

Many women marry men in order to be taken care of emotionally. A woman may want her husband to be a "daddy." And that might work, in "regular" families—where husbands and wives know *how* to be adults, children, mommies and daddies to each other, at different times.

But that doesn't work in alcoholic families.

It gets all twisted. Wives take care of husbands who drink—most of the time. Then, they get accused of "controlling." But the wife thinks it keeps her husband halfway grateful.

They both know how very dependent he really is.

And she is afraid of his "taking his dependence elsewhere" if she doesn't meet his bottomless needs.

Ironically, one of his greatest needs is to feel like *he* is the one who is taking care of *her*. So she needs to fill *that* need *too* she thinks, or he will find someone else to make him "feel like a man."

But a real problem arises here, because it's *all* an illusion. And they both know it. If he were really *being* strong and responsible, he would be able to carry his share of the load. But he can't. His sickness prevents him from doing so. And the wife gets mad, frustrated, depressed, and she begins to despair. How can she keep on pretending he's so terrific, so strong—and still keep the lid on her anger about the lie she's preserving because she's scared of losing him? And she feels angrier *at herself* for feeling scared of losing him and for feeling so mixed-up about it all.

It is really tough for her when she's in therapy or a recovery program and she is told to refuse to carry his share any more. And that means she's got to stop pretending he's doing more than he is. And she is scared, because she believes he might *not want* to really get well. And then he will find another woman who will build up his ego, pick up his pieces, and clean up his life.

So, this becomes another problem to the wife. *She is threatened enough by the sickness. Now she's being asked to take more risks, as she sees it, to help him get well. Isn't there any letup?*

What can help?

1. *Think it through.* The next time you get the urge to ask your husband for permission to do anything—something small, even, "Is it okay to go to the store now?" (This implies he will get lonely while you're gone and then get mad at you for going.) Think it through. *What will the result be if you don't go?* He will do exactly what he was going to do, maybe five minutes later. If he were going to drink or be mentally cruel, he will simply do it five minutes later. So you might as well go to the store and get what you need. That way, he will still do "his thing," but *you'll* be halfway pleased—by your efforts to please yourself. And that will give you more self-respect than if you didn't go (in order to please him) and he was rotten anyway. Then you would really have resentment!

2. If you ask him for permission, several things may happen: (a) He will make you feel guilty for doing what you need to do; (b) That will make you mad; or (c) You will also be mad at yourself for asking permission, since you really *do* understand that you have a perfect ethical right to go to the store without asking permission! And you could kick yourself for being so dependent.

3. Try starting out with making changes in this area in very small ways. A very competent counselee, Sarah, even told her husband when she was going to the bathroom! They thought it was a joke between them. But it began to irk her, especially when he started referring to it in public. When she examined

the other areas of her life with him, she saw the *depth* of her dependence. So Sarah started her "change" by not discussing with him any more whether or not she was going to the toilet. Not so funny when you think about it.

4. Try to remember that you're trying to fill a need in your husband that's so deep, so insatiable, that it's like a bottomless pit. Keeping him reassured is an *impossible* task. *You* cannot do it—*not if you spend twenty-four hours a day trying*. That kind of reassurance—that he's desirable and lovable can only come from something deep inside him—*and it will only come when he is willing and ready to get well.*

5. *If you are not exhausted already from running yourself ragged trying to please him, you soon will be. Constantly asking him permission is only a symptom that you're probably almost always thinking about how to please your husband—not in a healthy, balanced, way—but in a frenzied, fearful, wife-of-an-alcoholic way.* You'll be able to stop this trying-to-please someone who cannot be pleased by at least starting to *cut down* on the permission-asking. (Once you've started, and gotten some success, you will feel *so* good about yourself!)

6. If your alcoholic is one of those who regularly proclaims his "independence" by announcing he is going to do what he wants to do, no matter who likes it, don't confuse this attitude with what I am talking about in this chapter. I am not advocating defiance.

All alcoholics have it as a major symptom of their disease. *They will do what they want to, no matter who they hurt.*

This chapter promotes, instead, the concept of the wife living ethically. It does not advocate that she use her new-found assertiveness to smash her husband—but to stop asking permission to go about her life, doing what is good for her and her family. This chapter simply suggests that she act like a responsible, ethical adult.

Help me to be completely honest with myself.

29
Act As If You Love *You*

Make believe, and you will believe.
Get the body there, and the mind will follow.
Act your way to good feelings.

There once was an actress who was a very sweet girl in real life. She got a role as a very shrewish woman on stage. And she played this role for months until one day she discovered she "wasn't herself" any more in real life. She had "turned" into a complaining, ill-tempered person. This is a true story.

What's the point? You can become who you want to be by *acting as if* you already were the kind of person you want to become.

You do not need to spend years on an analyst's couch to learn the root causes of your problems in order to learn how to feel good.

Let me tell you how Marvin did it. He always felt guilty about not being the kind of father he thought he should be. He is a recovering alcoholic who was trying to make it up to his kids—to be what he was too sick to be when he had been drinking.

"I had good ideas about what a father should be. And I felt like a failure. When I said I'd be home, something always came up. So, I talked to people who were good parents; and I found out that they gave to their kids more than I did—their time, their patience, their full attention."

He went on. "I started to act as if I cared—even when I didn't. When my boy came home from school and wanted to talk about things I didn't particularly care about, I listened. I didn't want to, but I made myself do it. I picked out one afternoon a week in which we'd all do something together—and I kept my promises."

He continued, "You know, it felt really crummy at first. I felt like a big phony because my feelings hadn't changed. I still felt like a stranger to my kids. But I hung in there, believing it would change. A couple of months later, without even realizing it—it was gradual—*my feelings started to catch up with my actions.* I started to look forward to seeing my kids after work. I enjoy them now."

It happened to Ellen too. Ellen is the daughter of an alcoholic; she's twenty-three years old, blonde, attractive, and neurotically dependent on men. She's trying to grow up and break that addiction.

Ellen is Jewish and comes from a culture where many girls are treated like princesses. But Ellen didn't get treated like that when she grew up. She didn't learn to be a princess. Her mother taught her to be dependent on men in a neurotic way. Ellen acted toward men she would get involved with like her mother acted with her father.

Ellen went into therapy—for eight years. She read all the books and articles that told her to stop acting so dependent—that her behavior was self-destructive. And she couldn't stop. In this one area of her life—men—she was compulsively neurotic. She always picked alcoholics or addicts or "crazies" for boyfriends. And she believed she had to uncover "the basic causes for her insecurities" before she could ever change.

Ellen finally "hit the bottom." She'd had it. She couldn't stand herself any more. She was sick and tired of being sick and tired. She couldn't take one more rotten relationship.

She went to a friend who had a good marriage. The woman was a whole, loving person. This was the advice she got: "The only way you've cooperated in a male-female relationship up to this point is to always imply to the man: 'What can I do for you?' You must learn to turn it all the way around and say, 'What can you do for me?'"

And that was the crux of it all for Ellen. She had to learn to behave differently in all the little things. But they are really the big things. Ellen talks this way now: "When I get taken out to dinner, and it's raining, and my date asks me if I'd like to be dropped off at the restaurant, I have to stop myself from saying, 'Oh, I'll walk back with you,' when I don't want to—because what I'm really thinking is that if he sees how much attention I give him and how little he has to do for me and how much I'll do for him, he won't reject me.

"But I've learned that the men who are truly desirable want women who like themselves too. If I act in the old way, I get the neurotic ones again. I may lose a few, but that's just a sifting process. As I get healthier, I find I'm glad 'I lost that one.' So what do I do at that restaurant now? I say, 'Yes, I'd like that' and I drop it. I don't thank him three times for treating me nicely. *I act as if I expect it.* I'm learning!"

I asked Ellen how she started acting this way when she didn't believe she'd ever really change, or that anyone would ever want her, once she had changed. "I had to go ahead and act as if I believed wonderful things would happen to me if I behaved in certain ways that were self-valuing. If I had waited to be *convinced* that my behavior would make others treat me differently, I would never have changed!"

I want you to remember Ellen's story when you say, "This won't work for me"; when you say, "I can't do it"; when you say, "He will never change." Try it. It's like jumping off a cliff onto a featherbed.

Lord, you are at work in my life. Thank you for helping me to like myself.

30

Put Him in the Back of Your Mind

He doesn't think about you most of the time.
Martyrdom is not a virtue.

The spouse is as addicted to the alcoholic as the alcoholic is to the booze.

That's the heart of the sickness of the family.

The next time you cry out in exasperation: *"Why* can't he stop?!"—ask yourself: "Why can't *I* stop—thinking about, worrying about, fretting about, feeling guilty about, and being angry toward—the alcoholic?" Try doing it for one whole day. You will find it's almost impossible at first. (Experts still aren't quite sure which is the greater need—the alcoholic's need for booze or the spouse's need to worry about the alcoholic.)

This is not intended to make you "excuse" him from his drinking and lack of responsibility towards his family. Oh, no! This is not another pity-the-poor-alcoholic essay. What I am trying to do is show you that *you* have a problem: your own addiction to your spouse. I believe I know why you think you *cannot* take your eyes off him: *if you do, you think he will get worse, pass out on the street, die, or behave in an even more obnoxious and cruel way.* Even though he has yelled at you to stop nagging him and get off his back, he has probably encouraged you to keep centered around him by his subtle, and sometimes not-so-subtle threats of what he will do if you *don't* revolve around him!

Examples: 1. "Get off that phone. You're always on the phone," he yells. (What is really happening: You've listened to his drunken talk all evening and you need a break. You can't leave the house, you think, so you call a girlfriend. He complains that you're not sitting there listening to him, paying attention to only him—even though while you're on the phone, you're *still* listening to him.)

2. "If you go to lunch with your friends, I might get real sick and pass out or die. You've got to stay here and take care of me. *I need you.* You're *so* good. You're my lifeline, honey."

3. "Stop trying to run my life! You can't tell me what to do! No one can! I'm *not* taking you with me!" Then you say, "Okay, go ahead and make your own plans." He responds, "You're going out? You're not waiting home for me? What's the matter? Don't you love me? I *know* I said leave me alone, but you know I didn't mean it. Come on; come along with me. I won't do anything wrong there, like I used to." So, you drop your plans, and tag along with him,

138

afraid to displease him. Then, when you get there, he does it again, and you get furious. You yell, you cry. He tells you to let him alone. "You're always on my back. Next time, stay home," he yells. You're terribly depressed. But you're glad you went. *After all, he might have done worse, if you weren't there to watch.*

That last sentence is the main way the alcoholic hooks his spouse. He *gets* her to keep centered around him—and then *he blames her for "keeping an eye" on him. He arranges all this so he can have someone to blame, so he can continue to drink.*

What does this "game" accomplish? It makes the alcoholic feel bigger and bigger, like a tin god, at the expense of the spouse, who feels smaller, and smaller, and the more she feels he is so very powerful to control her, the less control she has of her own life. Why does the alcoholic do this? He feels so rotten, so out of control of his own life, instead of turning inward, and seeing what he can do to make himself feel better, he thinks he can feel better by smashing someone else. Then, he feels *temporarily* better. But it doesn't last. That "puffed-up" feeling he gets into, that arrogance he puts on when he smashes her again, only lasts a little while. Then he sinks low again. This makes him feel he needs to do it again, and again, and again. That's why he acts so cruelly—ten, twelve, twenty times a day.

What effect does this have on the spouse? She feels like a crazy yo-yo.

One minute he's hurting her; the next, he's crying and apologizing; then, he does it all over again. And again. And again. This goes on for months, years.

What would happen to you, the spouse, and your alcoholic, if you stopped paying attention to his sickness? If you put him in the back of your mind?

1. He might get so scared that no one will rescue him if he gets very sick that he will decide to get help.

2. He won't act any worse in his cruelty than he did before. It will just be more of his "junk." Despite his threats, he's very afraid of losing you: much more than you are afraid of losing him.

Incidentally, there is a paradox here. If you would carry out all the things he "wants" you to do: drop your friends; move out to the country; give away your children (or just stop paying any attention to them and center around him, all the time, instead); live on a desert island with him—it's *then* that he will become *most* contemptuous of you, and possibly leave you: when you've dropped *everything* else in the world for him.

"Him leave *me*? How degrading. To be rejected by a reject." See how sick everyone's thinking gets?

Try to remember that you never "had" him in the first place.

No one "has" an alcoholic. The illness has him. Unless he gets truly well, you're living in an illusion to believe that you *can* come first before the disease. *No one is that powerful that they can come first before the needs of an addiction.*

That's the crux of the matter. You only think about him so much because you want him to place you first too. If you believed, really believed that you will never come first to him as long as he stays sick, then you would probably give up trying. Please understand that this is not personal on his part. The nature of alcoholism demands that the alcoholic place his family last—after alcohol and all its demands.

Believe this. It's reality. It's hard to hear, but if you choose not to, then you can beat your head against that brick wall for the next twenty years. Or you can try these methods to start living your life in a different way, and learn to teach yourself to stop thinking about him all the time.

1. Remember that he will have more contempt for you if you continue revolving around him.

2. Share your new-found knowledge of this family disease called alcoholism with a person who is suffering the way you did. Let her read your book; help her to find an Al-Anon meeting for the families of alcoholics; teach *her* how to cope. You'll hear yourself talking; it will reinforce you in your growth.

3. Start doing things to get self-centered, in the good sense. Learn about yourself and stay aware of who you are. Stop making yourself so vulnerable to other people. *(This way, you'll learn, in a roundabout way how not to make yourself vulnerable to your spouse.)* Really stop yourself from "putting your guts on the table" to people who will step on them. It

will be tough at first. But after you've learned how to do it, you'll feel so much stronger. If you're the type who "opens up" so much she gets hurt all the time, make a real effort to be less open. Many spouses of alcoholics have this problem.

4. Be good to yourself every day. Do at least one thing daily, for one-half hour, that makes you feel pampered.

5. Get into your talent. Most people have creative talents or gifts that remain undeveloped. Find out what yours are. Draw, paint, sculpt, weave. Do pottery, crafts; find a calming, absorbing, active, pastime that allows you to *expand*—that enables you to begin to find *your* center—*and stop centering around his center.*

6. Reestablish contacts with old friends. Don't be afraid. If you tell them why you've ignored them, how this disease forced your whole family into crazy behavior—how you have missed them, and have put off calling them for fear of rejection—you'll probably enjoy relating to them on deeper, more meaningful levels than before.

7. Get a job, if you don't have one. A part-time job—a full-time job—any job you can manage. Get out of that house and put yourself where you *have to* think about something other than that alcoholic for several hours every day. And keep that money for yourself. If you're married to an alcoholic, it's absolutely necessary for you to have an emergency fund—and fun money that you don't have to beg for.

8. If you have children, do all this for them. If you don't want them to grow up sick, become alcoholics, or marry alcoholics, change your household now. Behavior changes they see in you will be powerful examples of health they will learn to model themselves after. *Become* that parent you want to be. The results will amaze you, I promise.

Let God concentrate on you.

31

Don't Feel Guilty
When You're Mad!

Angry thoughts don't hurt people. (They only hurt you, if you "hang on" to them.)
Anybody who's normal would want to kill him.

This is not one of those preachy articles that tell you not to be angry at that poor, sick guy.

And it doesn't help you to hear: Your anger isn't doing you any good.

Let's follow through on some thoughts that underlie many counseling sessions that get nowhere:

"You know, Mrs. X, it does no good to be angry at him."

"I know." (But she doesn't really believe the counselor or care. She just wants her husband to "not get away with any more of his abusive behavior." So she screams and yells. What else?)

"Mrs. X, if it's so terrible, why don't you leave? Why do you keep taking it?!"

"I don't know. You're right." (That's as silly

as asking the alcoholic why he drinks. She stays because, right now, anyway, she *needs* to.)

"Mrs. X, don't you know that your anger is just hurting you?"

"I guess so." (Big deal. It hurts *him* more. And that's what matters.)

Mrs. X walks out of there even more depressed than when she went in. She feels the counselor's despair and frustration. It just makes her think her situation is as despairing as she thought before she went to see a counselor. But now she thinks she's nuts too. It's been confirmed by a professional.

Many counselors do this. Unfortunately, sometimes, wives of alcoholics go to counselors who don't have one inkling of the dynamics of an alcoholic household—or what advice to give the wife. They can't understand her feeling so stuck with him; with her anger—and yet she *stays* in that situation.

The answer? Simple. The wife of the alcoholic is as addicted to the alcoholic as the alcoholic is addicted to the booze. That's why she stays.

And that's why she's so angry. She's mad at him— and at herself—for staying. And at herself for being so *scared* to leave him that she thinks she will just die if she goes.

Why is it so important for the wife to deal with her anger? (Notice I didn't say, "Stop being angry." I said, "Deal with it.")

If you don't deal with your anger, you'll very possibly stay stuck in your situation.

What does "deal with it" mean?

1. *Accept your anger*. It's totally okay—and you'd be abnormal if you weren't angry under these circumstances. It's a sign of *your* health that you are angry for being treated the way you are.

2. Accepting your anger means dropping your guilt about it. If you did anything "wrong," it was not your "being mean" to the alcoholic. It was, instead, your babying him and putting up with his junk.

3. Go beyond your anger, once you've accepted it as being okay for *yourself*. What happens if you don't? You go from "pity" to "punish" and back again. How does that work?

You get mad at him. You yell, you strike out. He blows up. Drinks. You yell more. He "remorses" (cries like a baby and tells you how rotten he is). You feel sorry for him, and feel rotten about how "bad you made him feel" (the "pity him" stage). Next minute—he's back, doing it again! You get furious all over again. It just goes on and on.

What would happen if you stopped yelling, hitting, screaming? You'd stop feeling guilty because you didn't do it. Not that you don't have a right to yell or scream. But right now, the main problem that's keeping you from doing what's good for you is your guilt from feeling you're rotten to him. Do everything you can to eliminate that guilt so you can get on with becoming a whole person.

"But," you say to me, "then he will get away with it!"

Get away with what?

Alcohol is its own punishment. What is he "getting away with"? *He's dying from alcoholism.*

Now, don't go feeling sorry for him! That's not the medicine he needs. *He needs tough love. He needs you not to give him tender, loving care. He needs to feel enough pain from his sick behavior that he will hurt enough to get help to live.*

But what do you do the next time you want to yell and scream? Remember he's not getting away with anything. And remember if you yell at him, then it's easy for him to say he drinks because you yell. Take away that excuse!

And what about your anger about his not paying the bills? Or keeping up with his other responsibilities to you and the children?

1. You have the right—and the duty to yourself and to your family—to *not* accept unacceptable behavior. Continuing to excuse him from his responsibilities because he drinks is helping him to stay sick.

Of course you're angry when he doesn't pay the bills he's supposed to! *But just being mad isn't going to change one thing. Just screaming and begging, like you've done all these years, won't change anything.*

If you are emotionally comfortable, let the bills go unpaid. Now, if they are the gas and electric bills, and if you, rather than he, would get most of the painful consequences of that, then I would pay it and be comfortable in my own home. But, if it's a bill *he* incurred and it's something that would hurt him, not you, let it go.

And think about dropping your anger, after you've made constructive changes. Because all it does is tear up *your* stomach. It gives *you* migraines. It gives *you* a spastic colon or colitis. Or chronic gynecological problems. While *he* lays there, passed out under his anesthesia, oblivious.

Guide me not to neglect my own duty to myself while taking on the responsibility for another.

32
Forget His Bad Mouth

The word "neurosis" has been defined as stupid behavior by a person who is not stupid.
If Florence Nightingale were married to an alcoholic, he'd tell her she was a lousy nurse. And he'd have her believing it.
Silence can be a helpful tool.

Sandie sat in my living room, finally peaceful, after many sessions of trying to drop her guilt.

The thing that reached Sandie was her fine appreciation of logic. She was a law student and really believed that if a person were doing what a reasonable person would do in the same situation, there would be no reason for guilt—except a neurotic one.

This "game" had been going on for quite some time: Sandie's husband, George, an alcoholic, would bait her—and by this time, she had been making a concerted effort to not react—until she would explode. The evening before she came to see me, he had called her from out-of-town, where he was working, and told her he would be working extra hours the next week, at a place that had been emotionally threatening to her in the past.

Sandie thought about that, quietly. She knew they needed the extra money; she knew that if he was going to do "his junk" again, *he would, no matter where he was.* (That thought didn't help too much at this time, though.) She also knew he probably would use the situation to play games, since it was just last week that he was doing his same "junk." So, why expect it to be different in only one week? She also realized that screaming, crying, and begging were all ineffective and that he was going to do his sickness, no matter what she did. She was weary by this time—a little uptight, yes—but more, just weary of it all. Her stomach tightened some, but she didn't panic inside as per usual. So, for the first time, Sandie, without too much effort, was able to be silent.

George couldn't take the silence.

He started, "You don't trust me!" *(She hadn't said a word.)*

He kept it up; she kept quiet.

Goaded for the fifth time, she said angrily, "Of course I don't trust you! Why in the world should I? You're not committed to me, but to your illness! I'm not saying you should or shouldn't do anything. That's your business. But, since you asked—no, I don't trust you, since you just did the same thing last week. I don't expect anything different. Why should I?"

He yelled at her some more, telling her that if only she "had faith" in him, he would stop. Well, having heard that one for umpteen years, she let it pass this time.

What was new? Uncharacteristically, Sandie didn't call him back, apologizing, since she realized she was not sorry for what she said; she was not afraid he was going to become nastier if she didn't call back, that he wasn't going to be more committed to sickness or "wellness" whether she did anything or not.

And she felt very little guilt.

She was just more *weary* of it all than anything.

That was a wonderful place for her head to be compared to where she was before.

What's the point of Sandie's story? It will take time, but *you'll* be able, like Sandie, to hear "his junk," feel weary for a few minutes, and then read something to refresh you and get to sleep, without worry, guilt and fear. It will take time; *but you'll get there.* Days, weeks, months of effort, starting now, using the tools in this book and whatever outside help you can get, will *assuredly* get you the peace you're wanting.

Give me grace not to take myself so seriously. Help me to become detached from my problems.

33

Don't *Say* You're Changing—
Just *Do* It

The alcoholic hears what you do, not what you say.
The less you act afraid, the less afraid you'll be.
When you "explain yourself," you come off like a
victim.
When you "explain yourself," you often don't
carry through with what you said you would do.

On a cold, blustery night, six people showed up
for the spouses-of-alcoholics group. Marsha was
the first to speak up. Dog-tired, she told the group
she had been up all night—again—till 5:30 A.M.,
"explaining" to her alcoholic husband how he was
wrong, how much he hurt her and the kids. He told
her all about his unhappy childhood and all the people who had "let him down" through the years. She
had heard most of it before; but some of it was new,
and she did want to hear *something* that would give
her a clue into the "why" of his drinking and crazy
behavior. "*Then*, maybe," she thought, "she could

152

help him." This went on and on and at five o'clock, she really thought she got him turned around, this time. By five-thirty, they were fighting again, and she got so depressed, realizing the whole night had been wasted—and again she had to go to work without sleep.

What shocked Marsha was that four out of the six in the group reported similar all-night sessions. When they weren't yelling, screaming, crying, or going into fits of depression and/or anxiety, they were "counseling" their husbands—trying to help them see what they do and why they do it. Two of them had been their husbands' "counselors" for over ten years. None had succeeded.

But all of them reported that their husbands liked these sessions with their wives because they "brought them closer together."

This was baffling to the wives. If they did no good, why did their husbands like them? And if they did no good, why did the wives continue?

The reason is simple: the husbands liked the sessions *because* they did no good. They were safety valves for the wives to "let off steam"—to get rid of their anger, fear, frustration for the night, in a talk-a-thon. And the husbands understood that if the wives talked, talked, talked, there would be no action.

Why did the wives continue? Partly because they really believed it would do some good. It also made them feel like they and their husbands were "close" again, this time without fighting, without being enemies. It was the only way they knew, at the time, to be on the "same side" as their husbands—with the disease, the crazy behavior, as the enemy. It was also because it was easier than taking the *actions* that were necessary to bring about any *real* change in anything. And, afterwards, when he "turned around and did it again after that whole night I spent helping him"—then it was easy to see *he* was "at fault," for the wife had been blamed and felt guilty for so long, she felt *she* caused it all. She had to attach the fault for his behavior back on him and this was one of the few ways she knew how to do it.

Why is it so ineffective to talk and explain?

Alcoholics are so used to being told off, screamed at, and "understood" to death, that the words fall on deaf ears. But, more important, the alcoholic only changes his *actions* when he *really* wants something, when he is given an *incentive* to change. Getting "explained-to" doesn't give him an incentive.

Why can't he listen to reason, you ask. Part of the disease of alcoholism is that the alcoholic is *very* selfish. He does what *he* wants, not what makes *others* comfortable *unless* it will get him what he wants! Counselors often agree: if you're going to stay with the alcoholic, and you want what you deserve (him to treat you nicely)—then you'd better make it in *his* best interest to do so. And that means he *has* to have consequences: if he doesn't treat you nicely, you won't do something *he* wants. If he does, fine.

In the group, Sheila explained how she used this method at dinnertime. "Just to annoy her," her husband would start a project whenever she called him and the kids for dinner. It was not a matter of just a few minutes either. By the time he would get there, the food was cold. Sheila decided to stop yelling and feeling depressed and she decided to *do* something. Next time, she merely said nothing, but took the food off the table. When he came to the table, it was in the refrigerator already. When he exploded with "What the hell did you do that for?" she simply, calmly answered that dinner was on the table when it was ready, and when everyone at the table was finished eating, the table was cleared. She did not explain, tell him that she was not his slave, or argue. She walked away. The next time he yelled again, made sarcastic comments, and told her that "even baseball players get three strikes before they're out!" Sheila didn't "hook" into his game by getting into a discussion. When you're right, there's nothing to discuss—and when you "discuss" your stance with an alcoholic, you usually wind up defending it, and then losing it or dropping it. Then you get even more depressed, wondering how you wound up back there again.

Sheila's husband showed up on time next time. He also had more respect for her because *she* had more respect for herself.

Start off with "small" things, with situations you

can emotionally handle, with situations in which you can change your actions without discussion. Don't tackle the "biggies" right away. Give yourself a chance to have successes. This is a difficult area for wives of alcoholics. You're learning to break years of habit patterns. But you'll find that there is a cumulative effect in all this: when you can do this, in some areas, all the other changes suggested in this guide will get easier.

O God, give us serenity to accept what cannot be changed, courage to change what should be changed, and wisdom to distinguish the one from the other.

34

Stop Telling Him How To Get Sober (Don't Talk to Brick Walls Either)

He will do what he wants to do, anyway.
He will probably do just the opposite of what you ask him to do—just because you asked him to.
Once you take your eyes off him, he will just revert back to his sick behavior if he intends to stay sick—so, it's a futile effort.

"It all sounds so hopeless, so depressing," Nancy told me.

"It is, if you take the short-range look at things, instead of the long-range look," I explained.

Nancy remembered, then. We'd had lots of talks about this, but as is often the case, it takes hearing something many, many times before you can really "hear" it. You're so confused, so panicked, so depressed so much of the time.

Nancy remembered how keeping in mind the long-range effects of his sick behavior helped her

157

very often get over her desperation feelings quicker. She calmed down, right then, when she started remembering the facts about alcoholism—when she started remembering that:

1. The nature of the disease means that he *can't*—even though he seems like he will and he often *says* he will—go on, forever, like he's doing. If he continues to stay sick, he will get sicker until he dies or goes insane. He *must* make a commitment to true sobriety—and stick to that commitment—in order to get well.

2. She is *truly* powerless over him and his disease. What does this imply? She, the wife, can scream, yell, be nice, be surly, whatever—and if she is truly powerless—and she is—then, it doesn't matter what she does. He will get well if he wants to and he will stay sick if he wants to.

So her having guilt when she yells at him for hurting her again is silly because what she does is irrelevant to what he will do. She can't make him drink or not drink. She can't make him compulsive, impulsive, or allergic to alcohol, no matter what she does. This disease is much bigger than both of them.

So the wife might as well save her energy. She might as well spend her time making herself happy and thinking of ways to do that. Life is so short! As Nancy wearily realized, whatever mood he was in, no matter what she did or did not do, because his illness made him so self-centered, he was not even that aware of what she did.

The only thing he was really pretty much aware of was when he needed, in his sickness, to hurt her emotionally. He was aware of when she was hovering over him too much and worrying about him and afraid of him. Then he'd feel really powerful and contemptuous of her, instead of grateful that she cared about him being so sick. So, instead of saying, "thanks," he'd hurt her more.

Finally, Nancy got so fed up that she just couldn't take one more minute of that kind of caring about him, any more. She'd had it. And that was good. For it did no good anyway. All it did was make Nancy sicker, worrying about him, getting scared, angry, fearful for him, for her. So, out of exhaustion, Nancy stopped trying to find ways to get him sober.

Most wives of alcoholics, go through trying to get him sober two, five, ten, twenty, thirty, forty times. Back and forth, back and forth, emotionally. From "I've had enough," to forgetting the pain; forgetting that his few good days *don't* mean he's well—forgetting it does him no good—forgetting her peace of mind when she could truly tune him out of her life for a while. Then, the fear of loneliness, her forgetting that he's an alcoholic, the fear that *she's* really the crazy one, the fear that it's probably true that he takes care of her emotionally and that she will fall apart without him—all that takes over, for a while and she gets re-involved with him. Until it becomes unbearable again. And it's over and over and over.

But you can make a decision—one of those

times—to get off that merry-go-round, that insanity-go-round. You can decide to *not* go through it for another month, year, or years.

Just knowing he will get sicker if he continues to do sick, hurtful things, including drinking, in his alcoholism; just knowing that you have choices, can calm you down a lot—the next time you get panicked, furious, enraged, when he says that he will do what he wants to do when he wants to do it.

Help me, Lord, to let you speak through me.

35

Don't Get Scared When He Threatens To Drink

At first, just act like you're not reacting.
The worst thing you can do is to let an alcoholic
think you're afraid of him.
You will get to the point where you just don't care
if he threatens or not.

Carolyn told me she never would have thought she'd get to the point of not caring whether he threatened to drink, leave, or do or not do anything. She had been making progress in a lot of other areas, trying hard to grow, get more centered, but she still needed to react to his threats. He would sometimes just *imply* that he would be in a drinking situation and that would cause her to burn with anger. She just *had* to explode, when he would do that. Often, he'd feign innocence by widening his eyes, and claiming he didn't think she'd be *that* upset by what he said, and he *certainly* didn't mean to upset her— and *of course* he wouldn't do anything to upset her.

And then he'd grin knowing he "had" her, knowing he could make her react to him as surely as a puppeteer pulls on a marionette's strings. And Carolyn knew it and hated him for it, knowing she couldn't stop.

And then, one day, the incredible happened. Carolyn didn't realize it, but while she was getting stronger in other areas, and despairing about this one habit she couldn't break, it, too, was unknowingly being whittled away at, very slowly. (The process of getting well is often a hidden one.)

One evening, she felt a peace, a calm, for six or seven hours, that she hadn't known before, when she thought about things that used to upset her. That day, she even had passed bars and liquor stores on the street. They used to frighten her. She didn't care. She passed people in bars, saw men and women, drinking and flirting, and didn't care.

Carolyn started to live her life in a way that *always* spoke to the alcoholic: I am not afraid of you or of your threats.

When he said to her: you only look good in black, and implied he would flirt with another woman if she wore bright colors, she bought a shocking pink outfit. If he said he beat up his last wife, she let him know, looking him dead in the eye, that if he *ever* even threatened to hit her she would have him in jail before the count of ten!

The more you act afraid of his threats, the more

arrogant he becomes, and the more he threatens. Conversely, the less importance you attach to his threats, the less he will use them, *because they will become ineffective.*

There are various methods one may use in order to render the alcoholic's threats useless. If being "passive," and not reacting rankles you—if you still react inside—you may be able, yet, to let it pass. The only way it truly works to let it pass is if it really doesn't bother you. You have other choices: You may make the consequences of his threats more painful to him than pleasurable. Whenever he threatens to drink, or to do anything that is hurtful to you and your children, you may leave for a few minutes, an hour, a day, a week, or whatever. You may do anything that makes you comfortable; that restores your dignity to you—that says to you and him, "I do not have to be humiliated and I do not have to live like that." You have the right to remove yourself from *any* situation that is painful, that is not life-enjoying.

You can call his bluff: You can really do it up and bow graciously to the door, and say, "Be my guest" and smile—or laugh! It is good medicine for you to laugh at threats. It will also take the wind out of his sails. If he goes out to drink, don't be there when he gets back. Go out to a movie, *get in later than he does,* glow with the good time you had—in contrast to the beaten-wife image you used to project. Smile; tell him you had a great time. Ask him how his evening was. Look sad for him, in a distant kind of way, when he says, "terrible," or if he bluffs that it was great. Then, look distracted and go about some business, like brushing out your hair, removing your makeup. Act like *you* are on your mind—*not him.*

As you may have gathered, *the whole idea is to take the power to hurt you out of his hands.* It is very bad for him to have that power (or rather, to think he has it). It will keep him arrogant. But, his arrogance-needs, his power-needs are his problem. Your task is to get up off your knees and stop begging him not to hurt you. Stop begging him not to drink. Stop reacting when he threatens to kill himself. Just start seeing him as pathetic when he does that. Brand this word across his forehead when he pulls those threats: pathetic.

For when a man with a fatal illness continues to threaten to kill himself for the momentary puffed-up "pleasure" of smashing his wife emotionally, he *is* a very sad, pathetic person.

Whatever your methods to stop being afraid of your husband—use them. Don't be discouraged when you fall back a bit. Old habits are hard to break even when they're built on illusions.

For God hath not given us the spirit of fear; but of power, and of love, and of a sound mind (2 Tim. 1:7).

36

Wipe Out Saying,
"You've Been Drinking Again!"

He knows it.
It's useless.
There's a more effective way to make your point.

I am not telling you to stop this because you are "nagging." Anyone would nag—and much more!—if they had to live with a drinking alcoholic for two, ten, or twenty years.

I am telling you to stop because it doesn't work. And you know this already. If it did work, wouldn't it have worked by now? After all, you've been telling him "he's been drinking again" for all these years and he hasn't stopped.

"But I'm so mad at him!"

Of course you are. If you weren't, you wouldn't be human.

"But even if it doesn't work, I *want* to tell him I know he's been drinking again. Because I want to let him know he's not getting away with anything—

pretending he hasn't been drinking!"

Let's follow this scenario through: You tell him he's been drinking; he gets mad, and denies it; a few choice words follow; both of you become furious. You call him a liar; he tells you to get off his back. He uses this as a further excuse to drink more. He slams out the door. Your head gets tight, your stomach is in a knot, you hate him, you cry, you call your girlfriend and say, "He's done it again!" She's disgusted by now, and repeats, "Why do you put up with it?" You wonder why. You may threaten to leave. You don't leave. You've tried that. You came back. It was worse. You hate yourself for staying. You are very depressed. Over half the day is gone. Again.

Do you want to go through twenty more years of this? "No, but. . . ."

I know you're angry; and you think that if you stop, he will just go off scot-free. But, you see, he already *is* off scot-free—he's doing what he wants to do (drinking) and you're the one left at home, with *your* stomach torn up.

What can you do?

First, you must understand that a lot of your instant fights are a result of habit. And habits are hard to break. It becomes a compulsion, one that is almost as addictive as his drinking is for him. But you *can* stop, by replacing your "telling him off" with:

1. Leaving the room as soon as you notice he's been drinking and you want to say something.

2. Leaving the house and calling a friend immediately (one who will support the change you are making).

3. Saying you've got to go and get bread, milk, toothpaste, anything.

4. Closing your eyes if you can't leave the room, and replacing your thoughts. Remove yourself from that situation in your head. Think of something you will be doing soon that will make you feel good. (If you don't know of anything like that, this is the time to plan it!)

5. Do not tell him he's been drinking. Do not make sarcastic comments. Do not tell him what you are doing.

What will this accomplish?

You will be putting the responsibility for his drinking right back on his shoulders. You are taking away his excuse that "you nag." You know, intellectually, that you don't cause his drinking, but in your gut, where it counts, a little feeling may say, "I wonder what would happen if I didn't nag—".Take away *your* guilt. It will be so much *easier* for you to tell him it's his problem.

Now, let's look at some of the reactions you can expect from your alcoholic when you stop telling him that he's been drinking:

1. He will be confused.
2. He will be scared.
3. He will temporarily be relieved that you are

"off his back." He will say, "Hey, honey, whatever you're doing, keep it up! It's nice to be home for a change!"

Your immediate, normal reaction to this? "That fink! How dare he act like it's been me who's caused all the problems in this house." Then you forget everything and want to start yelling all over again.

Hold on! Wait! Stick to it awhile longer. You'll notice that your alcoholic will start to miss the attention, the action. He will get scared. He will sense that you're starting to take your eyeballs off King-Baby, Lord Alcoholic. You'll be starting to focus on you and your needs, not him and his sick needs. He will try to get you to react to him—and believe me, he wants you to react. He wants you to go back to the old way of being upset by him, thinking about him all the time. But, you won't be doing that any more.

Soon your self-esteem will be shooting up; you will realize you can do things you've never done before. And your alcoholic will be set free to face himself and his own drinking.

Let me remain positive and rational when situations threaten to unleash negative forces upon me.

37

Don't Expect Him To Be Sober

He does mean it when he promises he will be sober.
He probably can't keep that promise—and he
doesn't know it.
The paradox is: when you truly stop expecting
him to be sober, he has a better chance.

Janice, whose husband has been in Alcoholics
Anonymous for twenty-five years, and who has been
a member of Al-Anon for thirty years, tells this to
people frequently: "My insanity was that for twenty-
five years, I believed my husband when he went out
the door in the morning and told me he would be
coming home sober. I spent the day half-believing,
half-fearful; when he came home drunk, I screamed
as usual, and fully expected that it would make him
come home sober, tomorrow."

What *can* you do? First, remember the facts.
Alcoholism is a disease; your spouse is addicted, not
from a lack of will power, religion, or love for you;

he is *addicted* to alcohol.

Try to remember that drinking is only one symptom of alcoholism. Another symptom is the alcoholic's desperate attempts to patch up his life by making promises he cannot-keep. One of these is his promise to stop drinking.

"Okay," you say, "now what? Then it's hopeless. If you're right, and he can't stop, I *can't* accept the fact that he will come home drunk. I could only continue with this marriage on the premise, the hope, that he really meant it—that he will straighten out. If what you say is true, there's no chance of our marriage even working."

Is there hope?

Paradoxically, when you truly stop expecting it, and start believing in the reality of his illness, start losing your personal anger towards him, get a distance on it all, *and plan your life for you*—then, your whole behavior, your attitude, your voice, your actions towards your spouse—all will change. He will sense that change. He will see, without your having to say it that the problem is his, not yours. It won't even be anything you'll have to discuss. Both of you will know it even though he may deny it. You'll have found your serenity; and he will have a chance to choose recovery.

Help my expectations to be realistic but never pessimistic.

38
Stop Checking the Bars

I know it gives temporary relief just to know—but it's basically part of a downhill trip in self-esteem.

If you can't stop it entirely, try to postpone the call; fill up your time with something very pleasurable, before you go or call.

Remember that you must be easy on yourself and give yourself a lot of credit when you begin to stop yourself, just even once in a while.

You don't believe this now, because it is so hard to imagine—but, you will get to a point where you really won't care whether he's at a bar, ever again.

There gets to be a time in an alcoholic's family—whether you're married one year, five, fifteen, or forty years—where you "hit bottom" yourself. He just can't hurt you any more.

One usually gets to this point after beating one's head (or his!) against that brick wall so hard, and so many times a day, that you can't stand another minute of depression and anger and fear. You really mean it when you say, "I don't care any more what he does. Just leave me alone!"

Now, you may have reached that point—and then had a "setback." You thought you'd "had it"—and then you turned around and got caught up in his junk again. But each time, the amount of time you stay hurt gets shorter—and shorter. *You get sicker, quicker, of his nonsense.* That means *you* are getting well. Never mind worrying "why" you seem to get so caught up again in his "stuff." As you get healthier— you won't be able to take as much of his craziness. *And that is terrific!* "Little" things you used to try to ignore (like when he was mentally cruel on a daily or weekly basis and told you he just makes "mistakes," and you believed him, and kept your mouth shut, but got very depressed) you just can't take, any more, *even if you wanted to.* This is all terrific. *You are getting healthier.*

But what if you're having a problem *starting* this behavior change of not looking for him in bars? How do you start?

Listen to what Cyndie, a patient of mine in her mid-forties, has to say: "When I first started going after him to the bars, I believed it was the right thing to do. He wasn't going to get one over on me! He would deny he'd been there and then I would catch him!

"But, then, I started finding him with women. Oh, it was *so* innocent-looking on the surface. They were just talking, but in a singles-bar-kind-of-way, if you know what I mean. Eye-to-eye contact, you know. So, at first, I tried to look like it didn't bother me. I even had a few beers myself. And then I felt really out of it, because I hate drinking, and I *couldn't* play the same game back with the other guys there, even though I was really tempted to, to hurt my husband. I guess I was just aching to get him back home and out of there.

"And then a new thing started to happen. When he went out the door at *any* time, I got sick to my stomach, scared that he was going to be with those women again. You know, they'd do *anything* for a drink if they needed one.

"Then, it got *so* horrible. If he wasn't already there, at the bar, I thought about when he *would* go—and how he would wind up with one of 'them.' And then I'd get so sick, it would almost kill my insides."

She went on: "I started begging him when I went down there. I got terrified of *any* woman, no matter what she looked like. And I got scared of every *man*—I saw them as guys who would encourage him to hurt me, so they'd feel okay about hurting *their* wives.

"And then, when I'd go in, he finally stopped looking guilty. Oh, he was past that. He just sat there and grinned at me, like a Cheshire cat. Like I was dirt. I hated him so much I just cried. I could have killed him. I threw bottles at him; I hit him, and then I ran out of there, scared that I'd get locked up. Luckily, the owner didn't press charges. He felt sorry for me.

"But I didn't go back there. I just called after that. And that was worse. Because when they said he wasn't there, I knew he was."

How did this all finally stop?

Cyndie hit "rock bottom": There was no way to go but up. She lived in a twenty-four-hour depression for months; she wanted to leave. She couldn't, out of fear that he really would wind up with one of "them." It was totally a no-win contest.

Cyndie was too tired, too depressed, to make the physical moves required to check him out any more. She called less, and kept saying to herself, "I don't care any more." And part of her *didn't* care any more. And that was the healthy part that was starting to grow in her through it all.

She finally got to the point of being able to "let go" of the situation *just enough* to be able to follow *some* of the suggestions the therapy group had been giving her. She couldn't before, because her compulsion to try to stop him from hurting her, and thinking that his hurtful behavior could kill her, emotionally, had immobilized her to the point of not being able, for quite a long time, to give up this chasing him, even though her mind told her the group was right.

But the group was patient. I explained to them, when some of them got frustrated at her repeated compulsive, self-defeating behavior, that *all* people were more vulnerable in some areas than others. "You will find that, when living with an alcoholic, you think that all he has to do is to find a nice lady who won't take his stuff in the area *you're* vulnerable in—and then he will get 'straightened out' by her. 'All he needs is a strong woman.' Or so he tells you. Well, I think you will find that if each one of you takes the husband of the woman to your right, and you trade husbands for three weeks, you'll find that the other wife's husband will find *your* area of vulnerability. He would throw away his old weapons—his old arsenal of cruel things to say and do—and learn how to 'get to you' right in *your* 'jugular.' "

After I relayed this information to the group, they stopped seeing Cyndie as weak, and realized she was dealing with an alcoholic who was just perhaps a bit more tenacious in his sickness than some of their husbands were.

We waited for Cyndie to hit "bottom" in dealing with his behavior and her inability to control him. And when she did, not out of an intellectual commitment but because she got sick and tired of being sick and tired of him, she started "giving up." And that was wonderful.

You see, when Cyndie was able to stop totally panicking, she realized *his behavior didn't get worse or better, whether or not she watched him.* And that was quite an eye-opener to her: she believed *before* that if she watched him it would be a deterrent to his going further in hurting her. And actually, it didn't matter one way or another. He did what he wanted to do, whether she or anybody else watched.

What Cyndie also learned, which was terribly important, was that her fears did *not* increase when she didn't see him "do his stuff," as she thought they would, from "imagining." She *didn't* fall apart. So she was finally able to take those steps towards stopping her centering on him, and able to *live* and *enjoy* many aspects of life, without the horrible worry, panic and rage. And those moments grew into hours, which grew into days, and into weeks and months. And Cyndie became whole, and peaceful, again. Yes, she had setbacks, but that's all they were.

The same thing can happen to you, if you're in the situation Cyndie was in—if you just make a decision to make *attempts* to get out of the craziness you're living in. If you just try, a little bit at a time like Cyndie, you will have no choice but to get well.

"Through wisdom is an house builded; and by understanding it is established" (Prov. 24:3).

39
Don't Beg Him To Stay

You're not as vulnerable as you think you are.

Don't come down on yourself because you're "the kind of woman who married an alcoholic" and who wound up begging her husband to stay. You've got a *good* chance to get over your vulnerability—because you can admit to it. Therefore, you can deal directly with it.

Why start this chapter off this way? Because there's often a lot of shame involved when one is very vulnerable and possesses low self-esteem. Why? Because "clinging" people are often the object of scorn by others who have a tougher shell.

Stephanie told me, "Many of the other women I know who are married to alcoholics tell me I'm so much more vulnerable to him than they are to their husbands. They say they can see the hurt on my face when I walk into a room. They can read me like an open book. They even get contemptuous of this frailty—I can see it.

"But do you know what? I don't believe they're that invulnerable. They just don't admit to it. One of them keeps herself so busy that she's just too exhausted every day, to even let the hurt in. But that's just running, not dealing. Another one screams at her husband behind closed doors—and then acts like I'm weird when I *admit* I do it!"

Stephanie has a point there. To deny you're being hurt isn't doing any good—whether you run or act tough. *It isn't healthy to learn to adjust to abuse.*

But what makes the "Stephanies" take abuse, and then deny it so much that they beg their husbands to stay when they threaten to leave?

It's simply a well-established pattern of denial and turnaround. She denies he has a bad problem; then she turns it 180 degrees around and says it's *her* problem.

But the pain gets worse and eventually it cracks through. And then Stephanie wants to stop it all. That's a good time to try these suggestions:

1. When he threatens to leave, show him the door.
2. Offer to pack his bag for him.
3. Don't raise your voice.
4. Remember that this will scare him so much that he will threaten he will never be back, or threaten to go to another woman. He will tell you you're bluffing, then go out and come right back, or go out and ask to come back that night. He will say he has changed his mind, and he may do all of this within fifteen minutes!

Remember, too, that it's very hard to lose an alcoholic—even when you want to.

I asked Stephanie to spell out her fears exactly. What kept her locked into this sick way of relating to him?

Stephanie and her husband had separated, but still she saw him regularly. *She* was the one who asked for the separation. ("It wasn't strength," she told me. "It was just that I couldn't take it any more.") But even though she was the one who had asked for this separation, she got terrified when they argued and she begged him not to leave her. He had finally agreed to stay, and then she had thrown him out again, feeling still more abandoned.

It's not as contradictory as it sounds. They both lived under a lot of illusions: that he was the strong one, that he supported her emotionally; that she was more dependent on him; that he had abandoned her, even though she had asked for the separation; that it was all her responsibility to make the marriage work; that "if only she had faith in him" it would all be okay.

Stephanie tried to double her efforts to get honest with herself in order to stop feeling so hurt. When she had facts she could understand, she seemed to be able to dispel the irrational fears more quickly. "Lloyd needed to hurt women—emotionally hurt them, that is—way before he met me.

"I used to think that if only I changed *my* behavior,

he would treat me differently. When I did that, it did mean that I didn't allow him to hurt me any more. But it also meant we had to separate, because Lloyd still had his sickness and didn't get the help he needed. Actually, he went for help, but he just wanted to hold on to his sickness more than he wanted me, I guess. I'd better not take that personally. He's had one other wife and two women he's lived with—and they've all had the same problem with him. Oh, none of them had my particular kind of vulnerability. In fact, each of theirs was different. But, he managed to switch tactics with each of us and "get us" just where our "jugulars" were.

"Lloyd knows all the reasons for his behavior. God knows, I've heard about his childhood enough. But a lot of people have rotten childhoods. So what? That doesn't give you the right to hurt everybody when you become an adult. In fact, if you *know* how much it hurts, by being so hurt, and if you're so very sensitive, like he is, you'd think just the opposite would happen—that you'd work real hard to learn how *not* to hurt people, because you know that pain for yourself and wouldn't want to have it happen to others.

"Last night, I told him calmly, that I couldn't see him for a while, not even on weekends, and I felt proud that I could love him and feel compassion and still not want to live in insanity. I was finally detaching! And then—two hours later—I was on that phone, calling him, asking him if he loved me, and I was terrified. I kept calling him back all night, begging him not to leave me. Crazy, isn't it?"

Crazy? Maybe to other people, but to anybody working with families of alcoholics, with people who try to learn to live in that insane world, it seemed par for the course, not at all "insane."

Stephanie and I talked about some ideas that might help her—and you:

1. Try to, from your head not your heart (from your mind making the decision, not your fears), make a long-range decision that will help you. If it helps you, it will help him. Then stick to it "against all pressures and persuasions," as they say in Al-Anon. *Expect* pressures, persuasions, and threats from your husband. They're all part of his sickness.

Do you want to be living like this ten years from now? When thinking about wavering from your decision, remember this question, and your emphatic "NO!!" will help you to stick to your decision.

2. If you steadfastly act from your mind, not your fears, no matter how lonely and panicked you get, in about six months, you *will* be a changed person. You will have started to love yourself, like yourself, respect yourself, and be able to love in a healthy way. You will be more able to sustain a comfortable relationship. You won't miss the excited misery. You will be repulsed by it.

3. Remind yourself that if you want to kid yourself into acting from your fears again—all you have to do is to tell yourself that "it wasn't so bad" or "I'll learn to *adjust* to it."

Things won't get better that way. You will just get more depressed and you will go deeper into your own denial.

4. Even if you could succeed in learning how not to "feel the blows" from his constant emotional battering—that is *not* the way to learn how to live. You owe it to yourself: emotionally, and morally, to learn how to get the most out of life for yourself, the best from all your situations. *And to learn to live like you are very precious.*

And even if you "learned" how not to feel the blows, it is not good for your husband to get away with being able to continue to hurt you. If a person is sick enough to want to hurt—to need to compulsively hurt others—it does not help him to get well to let him get away with it. That just drives him deeper into his illness. "Turning your back" on it, not responding normally and appropriately (i.e., not saying, whichever way you can, "you cannot do this to me") to battering, is your form of denial that it is happening. It just adds to the craziness.

5. You don't have to "settle for" anything the alcoholic chooses to hand out: cruelty, or crumbs of affection. Don't be so scared of losing someone who is almost just animal-comfort, by this time. If you act as if you're not scared, you'll wind up not scared!

6. Okay, he has the right to do as he pleases. But, you have the right to do what you need to do in order to make your life calm and peaceful.

7. If it's good for you, it's good for him.

8. It's okay and normal for you not to believe or feel any of this, yet. You will. You don't now only because you've been believing the distortions and lies of alcoholism for so long.

9. Alcoholics are told to call another alcoholic when they feel they're "building up to a drink." You must learn to do the same. I suggested to Stephanie: "Call *me* when you're 'building up to a call' to your husband—one of those 'fear calls.'" It's hard to break out of an addiction to an alcoholic.

10. When he calls, and threatens, remember it's the disease talking; that his words will change tomorrow—and his actions. *Don't be bluffed by his disease!*

11. Speak as kindly, and as little as possible on the phone, so that you can control your temper as much as possible. Because wives of alcoholics often get backed, "hooked into" him, when they've built up their irrational guilt by yelling, again. So, avoid having to drop that irrational guilt: by not yelling. Hold the phone away, and say, "Detach! Detach," over and over to yourself again instead. You're detaching from his disease talk.

12. When you "slip," if you do, and you go back to acting in the old way, *quickly* forgive yourself, and get back to your new way of acting. You're only human! Remember you're dealing—and you're new at it, at that!—with an awfully powerful disease.

If you're like Stephanie, and you've learned to beg

your alcoholic not to leave you—whether you're with him or separated—just look at learning not to beg as *a learning process*. Try the ideas in this chapter. You don't want to wind up two, five, ten, twenty years from now saying, "I wish I had."

Help me to take life one day at a time, and to conquer the habit of worry.

40

Don't Be Scared That He Will Leave if He Gets Well

Well men don't do that!
There's a big difference between "dry" and "sober."
If he threatens this, he's still very sick.

The ultimate threat in an alcoholic family is abandonment, combined with humiliation.

Very often the threat comes many ways. Everyone in the family labors under the illusion that the alcoholic is very powerful, very important, a little tin god. You'd better do what he wants—or you'll lose him. And—if you're *this* scared of losing him when he's still a *drinking* alcoholic—what a prize you'd lose if he decided to get sober!

See how distorted everything gets in the alcoholic home?

What things can you try to remember when you're starting to panic again—when you're afraid of losing him if he gets sober?

1. An addict who does not want to give up his

habit does an interesting trick: he scares you into thinking he will be *so* sexy, *so* irresistible to the opposite sex, when and if he decides to get un-anesthetized, that you might lose him. So, he gets you to help him stay drunk! It's like the woman who says she wants to lose weight, but really doesn't, so she makes subtle hints about how incredibly desirable she will be when she's thin, over and over. Her husband runs to the store and buys her a gallon of chocolate ice cream! Then she blames him. "How can I lose weight when he's always buying me ice cream?" she wails.

Don't join with the alcoholic in this old self-sabotage game.

2. Remember: if he doesn't get sober, he will either die or go irretrievably insane from a wet brain, spending the rest of his days in the back wards of a mental hospital.

I do understand when you feel you'd sometimes rather he be dead than "soberly" leave you and humiliate you—after all the years you have stood by him. Your feelings are normal; there's nothing to feel guilty about. I'm just saying you'll feel much less scared when you start to see him in perspective, when you start to see him as being very unpowerful, when you start to see *yourself* as a nice, deserving, intelligent person who does not need to put up with anything a sick man chooses to hand out in order to keep him with you.

3. This threat of abandonment is used by almost

all alcoholics.

4. You can't please an alcoholic. What you do is never enough. He's probably got you convinced that you're a lousy lover, a lousy mother, a rotten cook, a terrible partner in some way, a very undesirable woman, too pushy, a wet blanket, too loud, too timid, too religious, or a screaming fishwife. You've probably already started to believe him and this means you're trying *harder* to please him. This makes him even more arrogant. He's really cracking the whip—and convincing you that you're the one doing all the controlling! Your problem is only that you believe him!

His expectations of you continue to build. And you expect more of you too. Both of you wind up expecting you to always be strong, to always be able to put up with anything—to be superwoman. But he is always allowed to fail you.

This whole mess sets you up for failure, for feeling like a failure, for believing that you deserve to be abandoned, if you can't deal with him and his disease.

5. You may even start to feel terrified when he decides to get sober. You can't tell anybody because you think they'll think you're rotten, maybe for not wanting him to get sober—because it's hard to put into words, his subtle threats that he might leave you because he will "be too well" for you.

6. If he threatens by saying that you'd better "shape up" and accept his behavior just because he's

not drinking any more, *then he's not sober: he's just dry.* All he's done is remove the booze. True sobriety does not behave like that. *Sober people are sane people.* They don't threaten their families with abandonment just because they have stopped drinking. As a matter of fact, they do just the opposite; they are so grateful to their families for sticking with them that they try very hard to make amends to them for all the grief of past years.

7. Why do you believe these threats are anything but sick? Because you have lived with his sickness, his distortions of reality for so long, that you have come to believe them as truth.

8. How should you act if he gets sober? Certainly you should not become scared of losing him! Remember: If he chooses to only treat 1/3 of his disease—the physical addiction—instead of his whole disease—the mental and spiritual parts, the problems that make him selfish and rotten to his loved ones—then he is the one who will suffer. He is the one who is playing Russian roulette with his life. You can't go on for long, only treating 1/3 of alcoholism, and staying sober. He can be dry for a time, yes. But sober for life? He must learn to change his whole way of treating his family; that's part of his *sobriety* program.

9. *You have nothing to lose.* If he not only gets rid of the booze, but of that rotten behavior—you've got a nice, *regular* husband! But if he chooses to just get rid of the booze and continue to threaten you

with abandonment—it's his loss—not only of you,
but maybe of his life.

*God, thank you for helping me live more fully. I feel
you are opening a new life for me.*

41
Getting Help

After having lived with alcoholism most of my life (I was born into an alcoholic family), and after working professionally, in the field, I can say with certainty that it's much easier to make changes—to grow from guilt, fear and hopelessness into hope, calm and sanity—when you accept help.

I'm one of those people who doesn't know how to stay off the phone! I can't imagine keeping all my fears bottled up! Whether you're like that, or whether you're the type who needs to learn to open up, to trust, to get rid of false pride enough to let the world in to help you—you get whatever you need when you go after help.

A lot of people believe everyone is fairly accepting of going into therapy or counseling. This is not true. Most people still think it's an admission of failure, of hopelessness; that your alcoholic is right: *you're* the nutty one!

If you're looking to your alcoholic to tell you what's right and what's wrong with you and whether or how you can correct it, I'll quote from the Al-Anon *Forum:* "DON'T LOOK FOR YOUR IMAGE IN A CRACKED MIRROR."

Some people aren't able to go to counseling or Al-Anon because their alcoholics won't let them; others won't because their alcoholics say that the problem is all theirs (the spouse's) and they think that if they do go, it's an admission that, yes, the drinking is all their fault. Going to get help does *not* say that the alcoholic is right; all (or most) alcoholics will say you are wrong, crazy, or whatever—no matter what you do. So, go to help because *you* need it, not because of what the alcoholic says. Al-Anon is the support group you need. People who will cheer you, who will stay with you when you've been temporarily beaten, who will help you on to be a winner.

No one in Al-Anon or counseling will ask you to do one thing that isn't in this book—as a matter of fact, there won't be *any* demands made on you. The program is a suggested one, and the solutions will be yours to make, when and if you want to make them. The people in Al-Anon know your hurts and they want to help you climb out of this mess—your way, slowly, and when *you're* ready.

Many people come into Al-Anon feeling angry, abandoned by a God they feel no longer exists. They think religion is a cruel joke. Although Al-Anon is not a religious organization, it does encourage you to trust in a power greater than yourself.

Be good to yourself. Get help and let some others take care of you; let others be kind to you; let others gently help you do things you've never been able to do before.

If Al-Anon is not possible for you, see a counselor or a therapist; join another helping group.

You've tried it alone up to now. Has it helped?

"Do not pray for easy lives. Pray to be stronger. . . . Do not pray for tasks equal to your powers. Pray for powers equal to your tasks." (Phillips Brooks)

APPENDIX A

Sex and Alcoholism

Sex and alcoholism: they're almost a contradiction in terms.

If he has not passed out, he is frantically trying to prove he is potent, even when he is obviously exhausted. Or he is so selfish, he always wants you to perform oral sex. Or when he does sometimes focus on *you,* it's so mechanical that you get depressed. You wish he could just *relax* and enjoy sex—and you. All you want to do is cry; you're depressed much of the time, especially after supper.

You begin to suspect that he's as compulsive about sex as he is about booze. Perhaps you've tried to talk with him about it, since it does involve you. Whereas you may have been able to achieve some detachment from drinking, its hard to become detached from the sexual relationship. All he does when you approach him to talk—is withdraw. He either stalks out, barks at you, or worse, he mumbles "he will do better." Or maybe you just get the silent treatment.

Maybe you didn't bring it up at all. You might be too scared to talk about it, thinking it will drive him to someone else. After all, *he* seems satisfied, you reason.

Sex is usually the last part of the relationship to break down—the last stronghold of denial. "If that goes, where will my marriage be?"

It's not just that he throws up, passes out, and is impotent—most wives would not get so depressed, so enraged at that. They would feel sorry for him. Why they get so *angry* is that it is all accompanied by such selfishness, threats of other women (real or imagined by him) and hostility.

It never gets better, except for a day or two. There's no letup; and, in bed, he tells you to "forget the past" (as if "the past" were really gone).

But *you* can't ignore your feelings. And you shouldn't.

Here are some case studies of women who have faced this dilemma. The discussion that follows shows how they learned to deal with the situation.

Karen:
Karen's Danny wasn't cruel or heartless; he was a sweet "boy," as she fondly thought of him. She had trouble thinking of him as a man, even though he was twenty-six. They had no trouble communicating on the mental or spiritual levels. But when he drank, which was often, he was so terribly insecure that he

couldn't ever "get into" sex. It seemed to be such an *effort* that it destroyed her desire. Add to this her constant worrying about his depressions, drinking, and his "running from" their relationship in general. She was constantly crying, depressed and guilty about it all, because she knew he was sick and couldn't help it.

Sara:
Sara's Ken was just the opposite of Karen's Danny. He was a big, football-player type; thirty-three years old. Sara told us that when "she kept the romance out"—just got into the physical side of sex with her husband, all was okay, for a while. As soon as she wanted emotional comfort though, he wouldn't talk or touch.
So Sara tried a different tack. She tried to adapt to his way—thinking it would please him and then he would become more affectionate. She got into the physical side of sex, and then acted like she didn't want any emotional comfort either. She acted cold too. It was then that Ken slapped her around— "playfully," he called it. "What's the matter, don't you have a sense of humor?" he accused. Apparently, *Ken needed her to be uncomfortable and hurting: when she didn't hurt any more the old way, he was going to make sure she hurt a new way.*

What did Sara and Karen do?
   Sometimes, for Sara, it meant doing what made

her *least uncomfortable*. There are times when the wife of the alcoholic is too scared to say "no." She must learn to get the most out of the moment. Block him out as much as you can, mentally. Don't fantasize that he's someone else, or you will give yourself a guilt trip, and you surely don't need any more guilt in your life. Do speak up and tell him what you want. If he tries to stop you from getting pleasure for yourself by turning it into a way to scare you about his feelings for "other women," just remember he'd find *some* way to do this to you, even if you give up getting pleasure for yourself. So you might as well please yourself—and attribute all his junk to his insanity.

Karen got the courage to say "no" when she didn't want to, or couldn't have sex. She learned to initiate sex when *she* wanted it. She figured, "I learned I'd better go after what I wanted with him. He's so wrapped up in selfishness that I would have never gotten my needs met, unless it happened to coincide with a time when he wanted it too."

Karen and Sara both realized they weren't dealing with "regular" husbands who could or would improve their behavior through "communication." Sure, their husbands would sometimes listen and discuss, but nothing would ever change, over a sustained period of time. The sexual, physical, emotional side of the illness was part and parcel of the total illness.

So they learned not to feel the traditional guilt about going after having their needs met. They began to internalize the beliefs that the guilt of the wife and the selfishness and guilt-producing of the alcoholic are part of the sick lock-and-key relationship that goes on in bed or out. They actively sought ways to improve their lives sexually too, as another step towards health—and that was good for them *and* their husbands.

"Incest is the closet problem in alcoholism."
This statement was made in a film by a priest, a recovering alcoholic priest, well-known in the field of alcoholism treatment.

Incest isn't just the physical act; it can also include a fantasy life that distorts and destroys an entire family.

Now if you're thinking, "Wait a minute. Fantasy is healthy. What's wrong with thoughts?", then I say you must not really understand the context in which I say this. For in this book, we are speaking about a very special kind of family—with very special symptoms of behavior—a family whose father regularly lives in a full-blown fantasy-world, sexual and otherwise, with fantasies of grandiosity, sexual power, hostility—all which interfere with his functioning. He is not your average adult male who truly enjoys adult women. Rather, he "enjoys" the attributes of *powerlessness* generated by young women, girls, or adult women who will act out the role of a powerless child. He also does not really "enjoy" this girl; his enjoyment is much more an inverted hatred.

Often, an alcoholic, whether drinking or dry, will not actually try to physically have sex with his daughter or her friends. He will often, instead, play "games" around this, with various forms of seductive behavior.

But he often adds yet another "touch" to this scene: he makes sure his wife finds out about this. He makes his daughter into an unwilling partner in collusion with him: me and you against mommy.

What can the wife do?

1. Don't jump to the conclusion you usually do when you start to observe this happening; i.e., don't think *you're* crazy. I understand you want to believe it isn't happening, and you'd *rather* think you're imagining things—it seems easier to handle, that way. But denial isn't going to make it "go away."

2. Try not to blame your daughter or her friends. Children, even though they seem much more sophisticated than when we were children, are still children. Your daughter, as well as you, is the victim of your husband's behavior. He's her father and she is starved for attention—however distorted it may be.

3. Speak with a professional counselor about it immediately. If you choose to not go to a mental health counselor, see your clergyman or call the local clergy counseling center and ask for a person who specializes in dealing with this problem. Ask that person how to protect your children, not only from possible assault, but from the *emotional*

assault, which contributes to the family's craziness.

4. If you can do it emotionally, this is the time to leave. And insist that your husband seek, go into, and stay in counseling, and that you see changed behavior over many months, before you consider going back.

5. If you think you can't leave just now, still insist that he get help. Even if he denies that he has a problem, seek help for yourself to learn how to stay intact emotionally. And get the children to counseling too—even if they say they don't want to go. You make them go to school even when they don't want to, don't you?

6. Remember that the sexual relationship is the most intimate of all human relationships. If the alcoholic is "messed up" in almost every other area of his life, why expect different behavior here? In fact, it is logical that he will act even more crazy here, since a mature sexual attitude demands much more sanity than surface relationships do.

7. But, don't let that attitude relax you into "putting up" with it. Remember, it is truly *his* problem, *and not a reflection on your desirability.*

APPENDIX B

A Quick Test:

Are You an Alcoholic?

YES   *NO*

1. Do you lose time from work due to drinking?
2. Is drinking making your home life unhappy?
3. Do you drink because you are shy with other people?
4. Is drinking affecting your reputation?
5. Have you ever felt remorse after drinking?
6. Have you gotten into financial difficulties as a result of drinking?
7. Do you turn to lower companions and an inferior environment when drinking?
8. Does your drinking make you careless of your family's welfare?
9. Has your ambition decreased since drinking?
10. Do you crave a drink at a definite time daily?
11. Do you want a drink the next morning?

12. Does drinking cause you to have difficulty in sleeping?
13. Has your efficiency decreased since drinking?
14. Is drinking jeopardizing your job?
15. Do you drink to escape from worries or trouble?
16. Do you drink alone?
17. Have you ever had a complete loss of memory as a result of drinking?
18. Has your physician ever treated you for drinking?
19. Do you drink to build up your self-confidence?
20. Have you ever been to a hospital or institution on account of drinking?

If you answer yes to any *one* of the questions, there is a definite warning that you may have problems with alcohol.

If you answer yes to any *two*, the chances are that you have a problem.

If you answer yes to *three* or more, you definitely have a problem with alcohol.

APPENDIX C

Suggested Reading:

Kimball, Bonnie-Jean. *Alcoholic Woman's Mad, Mad World of Denial and Mind Games*. Centre City, Mn.: Hazelden, 1978.

Walker, Lenore. *The Battered Woman*. New York: Harper & Row, 1979.

Martin. *Alcohol and the Family: Three Sure Ways To Solve the Problem*. Liguori, Mo.: Liguori Pubns., 1978.

Dyer, Dr. Wayne. *Pulling Your Own Strings*. New York: Avon Books, 1978.

Weekes, Claire. *Hope and Help for Your Nerves*. New York: Hawthorn, 1968.

Beecher, Willard and Marguerite. *Beyond Success and Failure*. 1971.

Nudel, Adele. *For the Woman Over Fifty*. New York: Avon Books, 1979.

Chesler, Phyllis. *Women and Madness*. New York: Avon Books, 1973.

Silverstein, Lee M. and Roberts, Linda. *Consider the Alternative*. CompCare, 1977.

Peele, Stanton and Brodsky, Archie. *Love and Addiction*. New York: Taplinger, 1975.

APPENDIX D

Guide for Help

If you would like information about meeting schedules, literature and other services of Alcoholics Anonymous, Al-Anon or Al-Ateen in your area, simply call Directory Assistance in your area code and ask for the number. They will be happy to have someone return your call and help you in any way they can.

The author, Toby Rice Drews, is a counselor and social worker and she is available for counseling family members. You may reach her at her home in Baltimore, MD, at (301) 243-8352.

For further information or a free catalog of educational aids, write to:

Narcotics Education Incorporated
6830 Laurel Street, N.W.
Washington, D.C. 20012, U.S.A.
(202) 722-6740

New from the author of

Getting Them Sober,

Toby Rice Drews:

Eight audio-cassette tapes—
"COUNSELING FOR FAMILIES OF ALCOHOLICS"

All new material, never before released!

Write to:

MARYLAND PUBLISHING COMPANY
P.O. Box 19910
Baltimore, MD 21211

Ms. Drews is also available for lecture engagements.